Potters

Tenth Edition

Potters

Edited by Emmanuel Cooper and Eileen Lewenstein

An illustrated directory of the work of Fellows and Professional Members of the Craft Potters Association of Great Britain

A guide to visiting potters in their workshops

A source for studying pottery in the United Kingdom

Tenth Edition

Individual entries in the directory have been supplied
by the members concerned

Edited by Emmanuel Cooper and Eileen Lewenstein
assisted by Daphne Matthews and Marilyn Kopkin

Cover - Aki Moriuchi, glaze detail

Photographs supplied by individual potters or from Ceramic Review

Book design by Ceramic Review

Potters

First Edition	1972
Second Edition	1974
Third Edition	1975
Forth Edition	1977
Fifth Edition	1980
Sixth Edition	1983
Seventh Edition	1986
Eighth Edition	1989
Ninth Edition	1992
Tenth Edition	1994

ISBN 0 9523576 0 7

Published by Ceramic Review Publishing Ltd.
21 Carnaby Street, London W1V 1PH
© Ceramic Review Publishing Ltd
Printed by Yeomans Press, Mayfield, Sussex.

Contents

Introduction

'Potters' is the illustrated directory of the current work of Fellows and Professional Members of the Craft Potters Association. Earlier editions have proved to be useful guides to pots and potters in the United Kingdom and an invaluable source of information on work being made in the UK today. This, the tenth edition, has been completely revised. Illustrations of potters at work reflect the current interest in the maker as well as the object and set the ceramic scene, placing the pot in its studio context.

The first section, the directory between pages 9-236, illustrates the work made by Fellows and Professional Members of the Craft Potters Association, listed in their alphabetical orders. For the first time potters have been able to select whether they wish their work in colour, and over 90% have chosen to do so. The result is a far more attractive and useful guide to their work. 'Potters' also shows potters in their studios, together with a brief description of the type of work they make. Biographical notes are supplied by the potters themselves, and photographs illustrate recent work. Workshop and individual potters marks are included as an aid to identification. The directory gives a good indication of work that is being made today. It shows the range and diversity of contemporary ceramics, and it also serves as a useful record for future reference.

In the section 'Visiting a Potter' (pages 237-258), names, addresses and telephone numbers of members of the Craft Potters Association of Great Britain are listed together with details of visiting times, showroom opening and so on - invaluable information for anyone planning a visit. Some potters welcome callers to their showrooms and studios and some allow visitors to their showrooms only. This information is clearly stated together with the opening hours. Many of the potters have indicated that they welcome visitors, but by appointment only. If you wish to visit a potter who can only see you by appointment please write or telephone beforehand.

'Becoming a Potter' is a valuable guide to a wide range of learning opportunities. It lists degree and vocational courses available at art schools, colleges and institutions of higher education and has been completely revised for this edition. It also contains information on part-time study. There is also useful advice on how to apply to work with potters in their workshops.

The Craft Potters Association is the largest organisation of studio potters in Britain and has 156 Fellows and 114 Professional Members. We are sure that this new edition will prove as useful a guide to contemporary ceramics in the United Kingdom as the previous ones. Every effort has been made to ensure that the information is correct at the time of printing.

The Craft Potters Association

The Association was formed as the Craftsmen Potters Association in 1958 as a co-operative to sell the work of its potter members and to increase general awareness of the craft. In 1955 purchase tax was extended to include domestic ware. This led Walter Lipton who was then at the Rural Industries Bureau to arrange an exhibition of pottery for export in a move to help potters; it was bought complete by a new Zealand store. This success prompted a group of potters to set up a working party to consider ways and means of forming an association that could organise similar activities.

Under the guidance of Walter Lipton the Craftsmen Potters Association was formed as an Industrial and Provident Society - Rosemary Wren was elected the first chairman and David Canter was apponted Honorary Secretary. The organisation is democratic; upon election each Fellow and Professional buys a £1 share and is entitled to elect Council Members and to vote at the Annual General Meeting. Policy decisions are made at Council Meetings when ideas from members are discussed.

The CPA continues through the nineties with over thirty years experience behind it, and with confidence in the future of the craft. Recent changes in the administration and structure of the association have brought it more into line with current practice. The category of Professional Member has extended and opened up the number of potters who can take part in this remarkable organisation, while the wide and inventive activities of the Associates have taken membership to an impressive 700. The establishment of The Craft Pottery Charitable Trust to further the educational aspects of the Association is a recognition of the importance of this work and the continuing need to educate and interest the public in the craft and to make information available to all potters. Equally useful has been the setting up of two trading companies, one dealing with the retail activities of Contemporary Ceramics, the other with Ceramic Review Publishing. All is under the watchful eye of the elected Council of the Craft Potters Association, the potters who give their time and energy to maintaining the democratic and fair basis on which the CPA was founded - a noble intent whereby the CPA continues to be owned and controlled by its elected members.

Contemporary Ceramics

The Council decided early on to open a shop, then known as the Craftsmen Potters Shop, to sell the work of its members in the heart of London's West End. In the Spring of 1959 a lease was taken on premises in Lowndes Court, Carnaby Street before the street gained its present fame. The interior of the shop and basement was built by a team of volunteers who worked in their free time for the following twelve months. On May 30th 1960 the shop opened with a superb exhibition of Ray Finch's stoneware.

In March 1966 the Association acquired larger shop premises in a building being erected in Marshall Street on the site of the house where William Blake was born. David Attenborough performed the opening ceremony of the new shop on December 4th 1967.

In 1988 the rear part of the shop was converted into a gallery and named after David Canter to commemorate the work and achievement of the Association's first Honorary Secretary. Major exhibitions by established members of the CPA and shows by potters at the start of their career are held in the gallery. The shop also contains a 'Collector's Cabinet' of work by early studio potters such as Bernard Leach, Michael Cardew, Katharine Pleydell-Bouverie and Denise Wren, all one-time members of the CPA, whose work is now finding a new and appreciative audience. 'Contemporary Ceramics' is unique in Central London selling and exhibiting only studio pots. The shop also has a well equipped sundries section which stocks sponges, cones, turning tools, cane handles, Japanese brushes, sieves etc. all at very competitive prices. A wide range of books on ceramics as well as international catalogues and magazines on pottery are on sale in addition to postcards of specially photographed pots. Fellows, Professional, Associate and Junior Members are entitled to a 10% discount on all purchases except books.

In 1990 the shop adopted the new name Contemporary Ceramics, the Craft Potters Shop and Gallery. Improvements to the interior display continue to be made, the latest being an enlarged Books section showing a large selection of current titles - an excellent place to browse and make new discoveries.

Association Membership

The CPA is the only national body representing potters. Fellows are elected by the Council and are entitled to vote at AGMs and to show work in 'Contemporary Ceramics'. Professional Members are also elected by the Council and are also able to vote at AGMs. They may be invited to show their work in 'Contemporary Ceramics' from time to time or in special exhibitions. Associate membership is open to anyone interested in ceramics.

Association Activities

As well as 156 Fellows and 114 Professional Members, the Craft Potters Association has an average of 500 Associate Members who contribute much to its activities. Many of the association's activities are the responsibility of council sub-committees. CPA Archives are under the care of Moira Vincentelli at Aberystwyth Arts Centre (University College of Wales). Evening meetings have included talks by eminent potters from both this country and overseas. A recent talk was given by Mo Jupp who discussed his wide and varied approach to ceramics. Weekend events are aranged from time to time, the most recent of which was the highly successful two-day Potters Market in June 1994. Publication is also well established of a regular newsletter for all members *CPA News* . This carries news of shop and association activities, a letters section plus articles by members. Associate members receive advance information of all events, priority booking, reduced fees and invitations to private views of exhibitions.

Ceramic Review Publications

The internationally acclaimed magazine *Ceramic Review* a contemporary survey of studio pottery, is published by the newly formed subsidiary company Ceramic Review Publications Ltd. It appears six times a year and has extensive circulation both in this country and abroad. Members can subscribe to the magazine at a reduced rate. Other publications are *The Ceramic Review Book of Clay Bodies and Glaze Recipes* (4th edition 1988) which includes over 700 recipes from professional potters and has much useful advice on mixing and using bodies and glazes. *Potters Tips* edited by Robert Fournier, brought together the many useful tips published in *Ceramic Review* over the last 20 years and was published in 1990.

Illustrated Directory of CPA Fellows

Most Fellows of the Association have work on sale at Contemporary Ceramics the Craft Potters Shop. A full list of Fellows together with their addresses, can be found on page 237

Lead Release

The Craft Potters Association is fully aware of the possible danger to health of cadmium or lead released from glazed pottery into food. The CPA Council requires all members sending work to the shop to state whether lead or cadmium are used in their pottery or not. If these materials are present then potters must have their work tested regularly and produce certificates to show that it conforms to the new British Standard **BS6748**. The public can buy safely from the CPA shop.

Tim Andrews

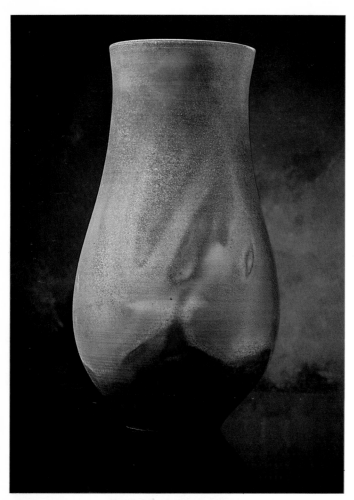

Tim Andrews specialises in smoked and burnished pots including raku. He favours strong classical forms with a variety of surface textures, impressed and incised decoration, fuming, lustres and other treatments. Trained with David Leach 1978-79 and at Dartington Pottery Training Workshop 1979-81. For a number of years made mostly domestic stoneware and porcelain (he still makes limited quantities of both) and ran a series of international summer schools. 1986-93 shared studio with David Leach. Since beginning 1994 working from own converted house and workshop in Woodbury, East Devon. Work is exhibited widely in the UK and Europe and he is the author of a recent book *Raku - A Review of Contemporary Work* published by A & C Black.

Mick Arnup

Mick Arnup has a fine arts background completing his training at the R.C.A. in 1953. Since 1972 he has been a full-time potter making a range of reduced decorated stoneware, architectural ceramics, numerals and letters. Exhibits regularly in the UK and abroad, often with his wife Sally Arnup, the animal sculptor.

Keith Ashley

Keith Ashley Born Yeovil, Somerset, 1944. Trained at Farnham Art College 1962-65. Studio at Farleigh Studios, Stoke Newington, London. Produces raku-fired sculpture.

Chris Aston

Chris Aston , who has been potting for nearly thirty years, continues to innovate new methods of making pots. When lecturing and demonstrating he now includes his latest self built press for producing slab dishes, as well as extruding Japanese style dishes with final shaping using wooden jigs to cut and form. His current work includes two main aspects, a strong core of repetition throwing producing attractive and durable domestic ware with distinctive copper red dot and brushwork decoration, and special pieces for exhibitions using textured lustre on delicately formed bottles in his favourite shades of reds, pinks and lilacs.

Felicity Aylief

F. AYLIEFF.

Felicity Aylief is a lecturer on the degree course in Ceramics at Bath College of Higher Education. Her current work employs a number of handbuilding techniques and her concern is with the archetype vessel form. She uses coloured clay bodies and achieves rich surfaces to her work by layering agate, sgraffito and inlay decorative techniques. Glaze is rarely used and a matt quality is achieved by high firing the clay to vitrification. Alongside this she is involved in research at the RCA producing a new body for press moulding on a more architectural scale. She has exhibited extensively throughout Britain and abroad.

Svend Bayer

Svend Bayer makes woodfired stoneware garden pots and domestic pots. These are influenced by rural France, provincial Chinese and early American stoneware, and are fired in a large woodfired crossdraught, single chamber kiln of some 800 cu.ft. Mostly the pots rely on fly ash, although the insides of domestic pots are glazed and all the bowls, plates and dishes are glazed and decorated.

Michael Bayley

MB

Michael Bayley Individual handbuilt ceramics, including dishes and wall pieces. Oxidised stoneware, mostly unglazed. Inlaid decoration.

Peter Beard

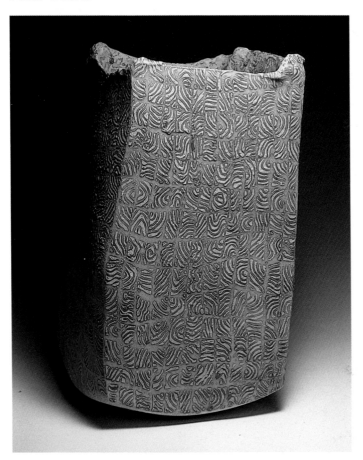

PFB

Peter Beard makes thrown and handbuilt individual pieces in stoneware and porcelain. The work is vessel and non-vessel based using glazes built up in multiple layers and wax as a resist between the layers to create pattern and texture. High and low temperature glazes with coloured pigments are used to achieve matt and fluid textures giving a wide range of pastel to strong colours. Exhibits in 'one man' and mixed exhibitions in many countries. His work is represented in many public and private collections. Regularly gives lectures and demonstrations and has done workshop tours of Australia and New Zealand. Part-time lecturer at Kent Institute of Art and Design. Council Member of the Craft Potters Association. Awarded various grants and scholarships for research and travel. A book on his and related techniques is shortly to be published by A & C Black.

Beverley Bell-Hughes

Beverley Bell -Hughes Born Epsom 1948. Trained at Sutton School of Art 1965-67, Harrow Studio Pottery Course under Victor Margrie and Michael Casson 1967-69. Work has been exhibited abroad and at home. My work is handbuilt and the shapes governed by both the making process and my interest in natural forms and growth. My aim is to get across the feeling of the material, clay, creating a bond with natural forms and being aware of the identity of the pot as a usable container if need be. I do not set out to imitate nature, but aspire to echo the process of nature.

Terry Bell-Hughes

Terry Bell-Hughes trained at Harrow School of Art 1967 under Victor Margrie and Michael Casson. Primarily interested in high-fired domestic pots thrown in series reflecting influences from Oriental and British country pots. Exhibited in several one-person and many shared exhibitions in Britain and abroad. Work included in several public and private collections.

Maggie Angus Berkowitz

Maggie Angus Berkowitz makes wall and floor panels of glazed tile. Work is usually commissioned, often figurative and always individually designed for a specific site. She enjoys discussing projects with clients. Recent installations include Hydrotherapy Pool for Chapel Allerton Hospital, Leeds, and panel for staff dining room in the same hospital; Great Urswick C of E Primary School, Cumbria. Past commissions have included memorials, games, heraldry and visual puns for offices, schools, leisure centres and for domestic use. She uses earthenware glazes and oxides on industrial blanks, quarries and ironstone tiles. Trained, taught and worked in UK, Italy, Tanzania, USA and Japan. Exhibits occasionally.

Clive Bowen

Clive Bowen The pottery was established in 1971. The pots are thrown in red earthenware clay and range from large-scale store jars and garden pots to mugs and egg cups. The domestic ware and one-off pots may be decorated with contrasting slips using slip trailing, combing and sgraffito methods. His pots are once-fired in a round (8' dia.) down-draught woodfired kiln to 1040°C-1060°C (less for garden pots).

Loretta Braganza

Braganza

Loretta Braganza trained in Graphics with a fine arts background. Painting illusory space on a tightly sculptured form is a continuing pre-occupation. Shapes are archetypal and are mainly influenced by childhood spent in India. The decorative slipware is a constantly evolving technique using a combination of coloured slips and underglaze colours. Works chiefly for exhibitions and commissions.

Carlo Briscoe and Edward Dunn

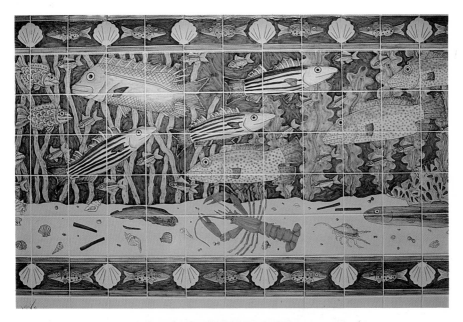

Carlo Briscoe and Edward Dunn have worked full-time under the name 'Reptile' since 1988. Make large tile panels for private and commercial clients including Waitrose Supermarkets. Also produce a range of mirrors, wall-plaques and ceramics which are sold through shops and galleries throughout the UK and abroad. The work is all tin-glazed earthenware and decoration is both painted and in relief. Recently moved from London to rural West Wales to a former butter factory.

Sandy Brown

Sandy Brown trained in Japan. Widely exhibited in UK, Japan, USA, Australia and Europe. Runs workshops on Intuition and Creativity; lectures and demonstrates worldwide. Work consists of: Inner journey; Clay Sculptures. A personal therapeutic narrative from Flying Figures to Goddesses to Lovers. Outer journey: Pots for Food. Expressive lively pots showing the tactile sensuality of clay with fresh spontaneous decoration.

Ian Byers

Ian Byers 'The preoccupations of my work are both poetic and sculptural, often drawing together ideas and images to create a mood and interplay. Most of the work is low fired and raku smoked.' Ian Byers is the author of *Raku* part of the 'Complete Potter' series published by Batsford, and has work in collections in Britain and Europe.

Alan Caiger-Smith

Alan Caiger-Smith Since the closure of Aldermaston Pottery in May 1993 Alan continues to use the premises as a private studio and shares it with Andrew Hazelden. The output is very small compared with the past. It is still mostly tin-glaze and lustre earthenware with colour and calligraphic brushwork, but there is now more emphasis on ceremonial and non-functional work than on pottery for daily use. As before, most of the work is wood-fired with offcuts from local cricket bat willows. Work is included in many public and private collections in the UK and overseas. Author of *Tin-glaze Pottery* (Faber 1973), *Lustre Pottery* (Faber 1985 and the Herbert Press 1991 in paperback) and editor with Ronald Lightbown of *Picolpasso's Three Books of the Potter's Art* (Scolar Press 1980) and of the exhibition catalogue *Aldermaston Pottery 1955-1993* with colour illustrations and extensive technical notes (available from The Pottery). M.B.E. 1988.

John Calver

Calver

John Calver I was twenty-two when captivated by my first contact with clay. Four years later I gave up my civil engineering career to pot full time. Initially I made domestic earthenware but, seduced by high temperature glazes, I changed to reduced stoneware. My forms are all thrown on the wheel and remain functional but have become progressively more highly decorated. The surface may be textured with fabric, clay stamps, rope or chattering; slips are brushed, sponged, trailed or inlaid; and finally, after biscuit firing, up to seven glazes are poured in partly overlapping layers.

Seth Cardew

Seth Cardew and his son Ara make wood-fired stoneware pots that are useful and decorative. The Wenford Bridge Pottery is run in an outward and forward-looking style, and has been in existence for fifty-five years. A collection of pots reflecting this history is open to visitors. Our brochure for residential courses on wheel-made pots is available on request.

Daphne Carnegy

Daphne Carnegy trained in France and at Harrow School of Art. Set up own studio at Kingsgate Workshops in 1980. Makes colourful tin-glazed domestic ware, thrown and hand-painted in the maiolica technique. Her book *Tin-glazed Earthenware*   was recently published by A & C Black.

Michael Casson

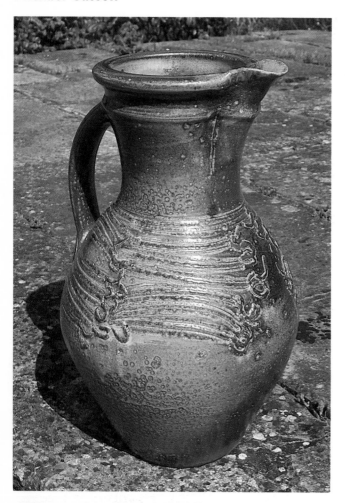

Michael Casson Early member of CPA 1957/58. Chairman early 1960s. Council member until early 1970s. Co-founder of Harrow studio pottery course 1963 (with Victor Margrie), Founder board member of Dartington Pottery Training Workshop; 1983 OBE, 1985-88 Vice-Chairman of Crafts Council. Books: *Pottery in Britain Today*, 1966, *Craft of the Potter*, 1976 (Presenter of BBC TV series). First pots 1945. First workshop London 1952-59. Tin-glazed earthenware. Second workshop 1959-77 Buckinghamshire, full range of domestic stoneware with Sheila Casson. Present workshop wood and gas fired saltglaze, individual functional pots, jugs, jars, teapots, etc.

Sheila Casson

Sheila Casson 1955 shared workshop with Michael Casson in London making tin-glazed earthenware fired in an electric kiln. Early member of CPA 1958. 1959 domestic stoneware oxidised in an electric kiln, subsequently reduction fired in gas kiln. 1977 moved to present workshop making individual pieces in stoneware and porcelain with decoration inspired by the Herefordshire landscape. The technique is a combination of sprayed slips with paper resist and sgraffito, biscuit fired and then glazed in a reduction gas kiln at 1280° C. Recently my decoration has gone more abstract. Since 1990 I am also making saltglaze jugs, teapots and vases.

Linda Chew

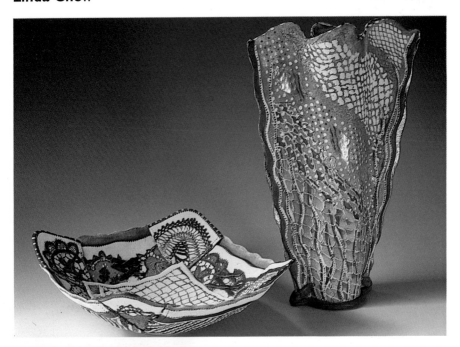

CHEW.

Linda Chew graduated from Cheltenham College of Art in 1973 with a degree in sculpture, from the Institute of Education in 1975 with an Art Teacher's Certificate, and set up her workshop in 1975 while teaching in Winchester. Her ideas are influenced by a love of textiles, the movement within their patterns, plus a desire to produce pieces that appear soft and tactile. Shaped slabs of porcelain and T-material are impressed with lace, haberdashery, etc. and assembled. After a biscuit firing, patterns created are then embellished with oxides and underglaze colours over wax resist, and fired to 1260 °C in an electric kiln.

Jenny Clarke

Jenny Clarke Trained at Farnham School of Art in the 1960s, and was influenced there by Henry Hammond and Gwyn Hanssen. Shared workshops in London for several years - including two valuable years with Ian Godfrey in his Islington studio. Now living in Bristol, where home and workshop are combined. Produces a wide range of domestic stoneware, using slips and sgraffito designs. Also producing individual porcelain pots using spraying techniques and brushwork for decoration. These are all fired to 1260°C in an electric kiln. Sells and exhibits at a number of craft galleries. Member of the Gloucestershire Guild of Craftsmen.

Derek Clarkson

Derek Clarkson has been potting for over forty years. Lecturing; demonstrating; exhibiting; full time potting since 1980. Works alone making porcelain and stoneware bottles and bowls by throwing and turning, firing to 1300°C with a reducing atmosphere. A range of glazes, currently being revised, and used including wood ash and celadon with cobalt and iron brush decoration; tenmoku; titanium; kaki and copper red. Some porcelain bowls have incised designs exploring graduations of translucency. Burnishing gold is frequently added. Recent work includes zinc silicate crystalline glazes. Represented in many private collections and public galleries including the Victoria and Albert Museum.

Margery Clinton

Margery Clinton studied painting at Glasgow School of Art. She began research into reduction lustres at the Royal College in 1973 and still continues this work. Author of *Lustres* (Batsford) 1991. Works with one associate Evelyn Corbett in earthenware and porcelain making tiles, pots, sculpture and most recently ceramic jewellery. Commissions have included tiles for the Middle East, new Glasgow 'wally closes' and Monument Mall shopping centre in Newcastle. Increasingly involved in architectural tile projects which she enjoys; the latest and biggest being the ceramic mural for The Mary Erskine School, Edinburgh, one panel of which is illustrated. Collections: Tate Gallery, Victoria and Albert Museum, Glasgow Art Gallery, Royal Museum of Scotland.

Peter Clough

Peter Clough I trained at Portsmouth and Manchester University, and have been potting both full and part-time for over 25 years. My current work tends to be thrown, altered and assembled, and I have increasingly used low temperature firing during recent years, with the raku process of particular interest at present. All making and firing processes are variable, and depend upon the ideas being explored. My principal formal concerns reside with notions of the vessel as object, as a metaphor for personal experience and biography, and with illusion and paradox. Senior Lecturer at the University College of Ripon and York St. John, York.

Russell Coates

Russell Coates Since moving out of London to the West Country, my work has changed. I now combine dolphins, sea creatures and a variety of birds with patterns which are derived from Celtic and Old English designs. I still use the traditional old Kutani colours - red, yellow, green, blue and purple on porcelain. To begin with the bones of the design are marked out with underglaze blue on the biscuit ware. After the 1270°C reduction glaze firing the bright glassy enamels are painted on and fired to 840°C. If gold is employed in the design it is also included in the enamel firing and burnished afterwards with agate. I aim to achieve a jewel like quality with the enamels in intricate patterns in the centres or in borders.

Roger Cockram

Roger Cockram Born in North Devon. Originally trained as a scientist (zoology). Postgraduate work in marine ecology. Ceramics at Harrow 1973-75. Own studio from 1976, at first making wood-fired thrown ware. Recent work mainly individual pieces based on marine and freshwater themes, sometimes with added modelling and referring to animals in their own surroundings. Also makes a small range of ovenware, pitchers etc. All work is once-fired to cone 10-11 in a small gas kiln and heavily reduced towards end of firing. Work sells through own showroom, galleries in UK and overseas; also through exhibitions and commissions.

Barbara Colls

Barbara Colls Born in 1914. Attended West Surrey College of Art and Design part-time over many years. Paul and Penny Barron and Henry Hammond were a great help in developing the bird lidded pots in which I specialize. I work alone in tiny studio, using stoneware and porcelain, all my work is thrown and modelled using coloured slips and glazes. Exhibitions at many galleries at home and abroad.

Joanna Constantinidis

Joanna Constantinidis Individual pots in stoneware and porcelain, also some porcelain tableware.

Delan Cookson

Delan Cookson I make individual thrown bottles, bowls or container forms in porcelain and am chiefly concerned with exploring thrown and turned forms, discovering endless variations on my chosen themes. Many are achieved by joining more than one section. I like porcelain because its smooth whiteness reflects all the brilliance of my coloured glazes. I enjoy working on my own and have been potting full-time since 1989 after twenty-eight years of lecturing in ceramics. Work has been shown widely particularly in the South West and is in many public and private collections.

Bennett Cooper

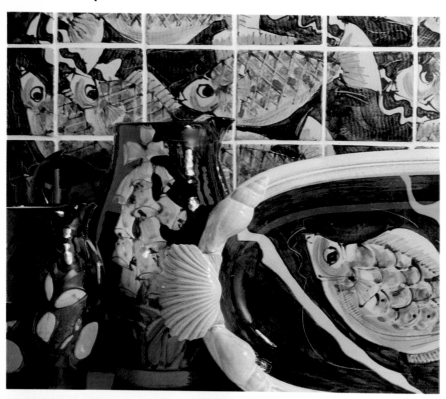

Bennett Cooper trained at Hornsey College of Art (Middlesex Polytechnic) 1971-74 and the Royal College of Art 1974-77. Set up present workshop in 1979. Working with high fired earthenware (1160°C) . I produce a range of pressed and thrown highly decorative table and ovenware plus a few one-off pots and some tile panels. Brightly coloured slips applied with trailer and brush enhanced with sgraffito and applied pigment enables me to work within the slipware tradition. The discipline involved in making decorative functional pots is a continual source of excitement and inspiration.

Emmanuel Cooper

Emmanuel Cooper Individual pots, mostly in porcelain, include bowls and jug forms. Glazes tend to be bright and rich and include turquoise blues and greens, nickel pinks and blues, uranium yellow. All are fired to 1260° C electric kiln. Has been making pots since 1965. Trained Dudley College of Education 1958-60, Bournemouth School of Art 1960-61, Hornsey School of Art 1961-62. Worked with Gwyn Hanssen and then Bryan Newman before opening own studio. Works alone. Co-editor (with Eileen Lewenstein) of Ceramic Review . Associate Lecturer Middlesex University. Major exhibitions British Craft Centre, Boadicea, Craft Potters Shop, J.K. Hill. Work in many collections including Victoria and Albert Museum, Royal Scottish Museum. Author of many books on ceramics including New Ceramics (with Eileen Lewenstein), Glazes for the Studio Potter (with Derek Royle) (Batsford 1978), The Potters Book of Glaze Recipes (Batsford 1980), A History of World Pottery (Batsford 1988), Electric Kiln Pottery (Batsford 1982), Cooper's Book of Glaze Recipes (Batsford 1987), Glazes (Batsford 1992).

Gilles Le Corre

Gilles Le Corre Born Quimper, France. Trained at Camberwell School of Arts and Crafts 1975-79. Currently working from his Oxford studio. Stoneware pots are thrown and decorated, some pieces are altered and reformed, all are glazed with layers of fused colours to enhance the functional shape.

Dartington Pottery

Dartington Pottery is located on the Dartington Hall Estate in South Devon. The original site was used by Bernard Leach as a pottery in the 1930s, and then by Marianne De Trey until 1981 when she moved to a smaller studio. The association between Dartington Pottery and Janice Tchalenko as a designer is unique in contemporary ceramics: the pottery specialises in reduction stoneware. The bright colourful designs originate from a European rather than Oriental tradition and in the '80s led a movement away from the more rustic styles that used to dominate studio pottery. Today the pottery is run by Stephen Course and Peter Cook and now employs about 15 people. Janice Tchalenko continues to be principal designer but the pottery encourages collaboration with other designers. There is a shop at the pottery and the work is available throughout the UK, Europe, the Far East and America. The pottery undertakes commissions for clients' specific designs, produces limited editions and tableware. It has recently developed separate design and manufacture consultancies in England, Finland, China and Bermuda. The pottery operates an apprenticeship scheme.

Clive Davies

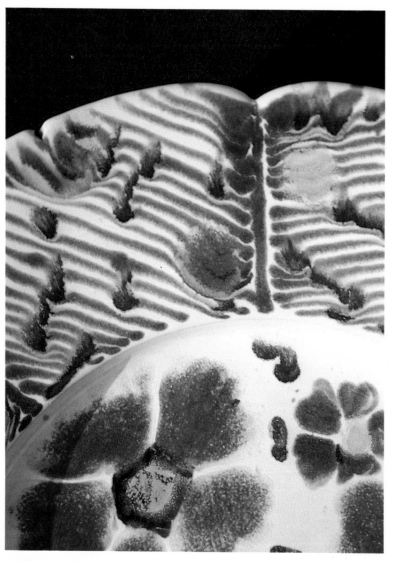

Clive Davies Born 1939. Self taught. Professional since 1970. Various teaching. Exhibited widely.

Mike Dodd

Mike Dodd Born 1943. From an early love of pottery, inspired by Donald Potter's tutelage at Bryanston, I decided to embrace the making of pots, after completing a medical degree at Cambridge University. I started my first pottery at Edburton in Sussex, armed with Leach's *A Potter's Book* and very little else. At that time my knowledge was to say the least sparse. I did not know how to build a kiln or even to throw a lid. Twenty years later I am involved with my fourth pottery and am perhaps a little wiser. The dignity, conviction and freshness of form, being the very essence of pottery for me, is my main concern - and I have a preference for using materials for slips and glazes from the surrounding area, which, this time, happens to be the Lake District, granites, hornfels, andesites, irons, clays, etc. In 1979 I spent six months in Peru helping the Amnesha Indians to build a large wood-fired kiln and experimenting with local materials for glazes - a great experience. My work finds itself into many and various exhibitions here and abroad.

Jack Doherty

Jack Doherty My work with porcelain is thrown. The surfaces and decoration are built up by adding stained and textured clay. Often the forms are altered while the clay is still soft. I fire with soda vapour to enhance and develop the clay colours. My work has been shown widely, including the exhibitions at Faenza and Vallauris (awarded Gold Medals in 1974 and 1976). Solo and group exhibitions in the UK, Scandinavia, Germany and the USA. My pots are in the collections of the Ulster Museum, Crafts Council of Ireland, Liverpool Museum and Cheltenham Museum. I am a Council Member and currently Vice Chair of the CPA.

John Dunn

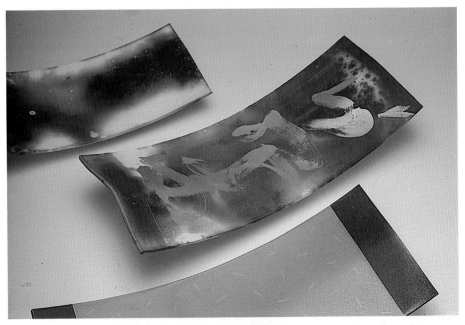

John Dunn I have for a number of years concentrated almost exclusively on the production of large raku dishes. Now I have decided to spend less time in this area to focus on one-off pieces using both raku and low fire techniques. Work is distributed throughout Europe and housed in both public and private collections. The workshop here in Brighton is becoming increasingly established as a training workshop offering intensive courses in both raku and low fire to individuals and groups.

Geoffrey Eastop

Geoffrey Eastop trained as a painter at Goldsmiths' College, London and Academie Ranson, Paris. Over a long period has worked through a wide range of techniques. At present making monolithic stoneware forms often painted with coloured vitreous slips; not as decoration but as an emphasis of character. Exhibitions include National Museum of Wales, Victoria and Albert Museum, London: Cologne and Stuttgart. Major touring retrospective: Portsmouth City Museum September-November 1992; Newbury Museum December 1992-February 1993; Holburne Museum, Bath April-May 1993. Architectural commissions include large murals for Maudsley Hospital, London; Reading Civic Centre; wall and floor tiles, Robinson College Chapel, Cambridge. Work in numerous collections public and private including Victoria and Albert Museum and Fitzwilliam Museum, Cambridge. Book: *The Hollow Vessel* Bohun Gallery 1980, Fellow Society of Designer-Craftsmen.

Derek Emms

Derek Emms Born 1929. Studied at Accrington, Burnley and Leeds Colleges of Art. After National Service in RAF worked at the Leach Pottery under Bernard and David Leach. From 1955 to 1985 full-time lecturer at North Staffs Polytechnic. Retired in 1985 to devote more time to making pots. I produce a variety of domestic and 'one-off' pieces in stoneware and porcelain decorated by engraving in the leather-hard clay or by brush decoration on the biscuit with oxide pigments. Glazes include transparent, celadons, tenmoku, chun and copper red.

Dorothy Feibleman

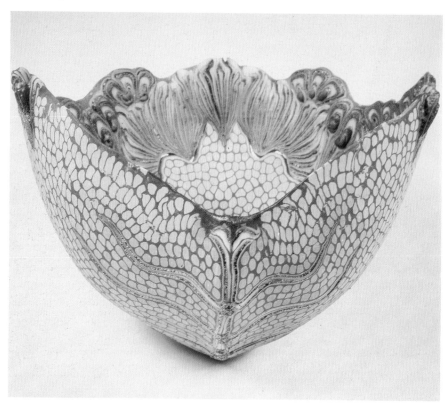

Dorothy Feibleman makes laminated coloured porcelain and parian ceramics including 22 and 18 karat gold and porcelain jewellery. Her fascination with using lamination is that the structure and decoration are integral. She makes ceramics full-time and gives workshops and demonstrations. Her work is in many private and public collections including the Victoria and Albert Museum, the Indianapolis Art Museum, the Frankfurt, Darmstadt and Stuttgart Decorative Arts Museums.

Sylvia Des Fours

Sylvia Des Fours came to England from Czechoslavakia in 1949. Trained at Epsom and Hammersmith Schools of Art. Makes individual pieces in stoneware and porcelain, thrown with handbuilt extensions. Teaches at Dorking I.O.F.E. and Richmond Adult and Community College; also at psychiatric hospital in Epsom. Believes in the therapeutic value of working with clay and is deeply involved in matters of mental health.

David Frith

David Frith Born 1943, has worked as a full-time potter since 1963, first making earthenware slipware then reduction stoneware and porcelain. Many of his pieces are on a majestic scale and an increased awareness and better understanding of the materials has brought about continual development of his work. Strong decorative motifs with wax resist, heavy overglazes and trailed pigments predominate. The milled celadons and iron glazes give rich qualities and research into clays and reduction glazes continues. The Brookhouse Pottery Summer Schools have been held for fifteen years. David gives lectures and workshops in this country and abroad. Past Council Member and Vice Chairman of the CPA, Index Member of the Crafts Council. Work in public and private collections.

Margaret Frith

Margaret Frith Born 1943, trained at Bolton, Liverpool and Stoke on Trent Colleges of Art. Set up workshop with husband David Frith in 1963 and has been a full-time potter since then. She looks on the early training as a production thrower of domestic ware as essential to the development of her present work - mainly carved reduction porcelain and coloured glazed porcelain. She has developed a porcelain body, made by the 'slop' method. The designs are mainly floral, drawing beforehand, but working directly on to the clay giving spontaneity and flow. Holds the Brookhouse Pottery Schools each year with David. Exhibits regularly

Tessa Fuchs

Tessa Fuchs Born Knutsford, Cheshire. Studied Salford Royal Technical College Art School, Central School of Arts and Crafts, London. Set up studio as an individual artist potter making sculptural pieces and some domestic ware in high fired earthenware using colourful matt glazes. Work inspired by her interest in animals, plants, gardening, trees, landscape and painting. She is also particularly influenced by her travels which have included China, Mexico and Kenya where she went on safari. Her latest work is on the subject of the human form. Lovers, Kissing heads, Dancers and Acrobats on animals. Also gods taken from the Greek myths.

Tony Gant

Tony Gant makes stoneware bowls, dishes, plates, mugs and vases. Established 1961; present studio since 1968.

Carolyn Genders

Carolyn Genders

Carolyn Genders My inspiration stems from various sources: my Viennese mother, my English father and my Far Eastern childhood. The peace of the gentle Sussex countryside and the natural rhythms of the seasons temper the strong influences of my past: the lush sensuality of the tropics, its richness and vibrant contrasts of colours and the textures and civilised decadence of the Secession. The essence of my work lies in these seemingly opposed, but, to me, complementary elements. Trained Brighton Polytechnic 1975-79 and Goldsmiths' College 1985-86. Established studio 1980. Currently teaching part-time, visiting lecturer. Exhibits widely in Britain, Europe and Japan.

Christopher Green

Christopher Green Thrown porcelain bowls and plates fired in a reducing atmosphere. Particular interest in glazes using iron and copper for colour, and in kiln control. Born and educated in Zimbabwe. Training in Durban, South Africa and Goldsmiths' College, London.

Ian Gregory

Ian Gregory Workshop opened in 1968 changing from earthenware to saltglaze in 1976. Elected to CPA in 1977 and served on the council for two years. Commissioned by his publisher to write *Kiln Building* in 1977 followed by two other titles *Sculptural Ceramics* and *Kilns*. Work is shown at Contemporary Applied Arts and many other galleries, and examples of his work are in many public and private collections worldwide. Guest teaching has been at Cardiff, Corsham and other art schools, and he is now Head of Art and Ceramics at Milton Abbey, Dorset. Currently producing one-off sculptural pieces, some of which are life-sized figurative work in low temperature saltglaze and raku.

Frank Hamer

Frank Hamer press-moulds plates and dishes which are decorated, often on the back as well, with graphic images taken from nature. The ware is reduced stoneware and all pieces have integral hangers for wall display or can be used as servers. Frank Hamer lives in rural Wales working in a studio which overlooks the Brecon Canal and where studio and kiln space are shared with Janet Hamer. He is co-author of *Clays* and *The Potter's Dictionary of Materials and Techniques*.

Jane Hamlyn

Jane Hamlyn Raw-fired saltglaze pots for use and ornament. Work in public collections: Victoria and Albert Museum, and Crafts Council, London, Nottingham Castle Museum, Hanley Museum, Stoke on Trent. Warttembergisches Landsmuseum, Stuttgart, etc.

Alan Heaps

ah

Alan Heaps In the early 1960s trained in Graphics at the Liverpool College of Art and has been making ceramics full time for the past twenty years, sixteen of which have been spent in his workshop in rural Mid-Wales. Each piece is individually handbuilt and decorated with slip and glaze stains using a matt glaze fired to 1140° C. He has exhibited extensively in Britain and on the continent of Europe and presently sells mostly in Germany.

Joan Hepworth

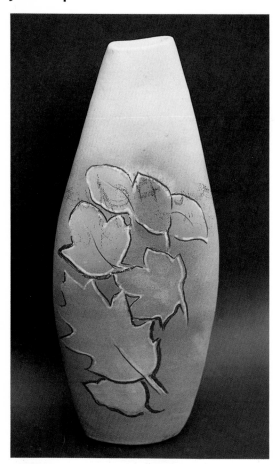

J. Hepworth

Joan Hepworth studied at Hastings School of Art for two years. While there won a scholarship to the Royal College of Art and entered the Design School to study mural decoration, fabric design and printing. After leaving college spent a year in a film cartoon studio before taking up teaching design and printing at Sutton School of Art. When pottery was introduced into the school she joined a class in her spare time and was taught by Harry Stringer and Brian Starkey. She became more and more enthusiastic over pottery and experimented with all methods of making pots. Eventually bought her own kiln and wheel and set up her own workshop. Finding she used the wheel less and less she decided after moving to her present address, to concentrate on slab pots and slip cast porcelain. Enjoys exploring and developing new shapes. Decorates mainly with ceramic crayons and some relief work. Uses an electric kiln firing to 1250°C. Finds the coloured crayons fade at higher temperatures. Has exhibited widely in this country with one-person exhibitions at Sutton School of Art and at Henley. Has also exhibited in Belgium, Austria and Germany and sold to Japan.

Karin Hessenberg

Karin Hessenberg I graduated from Camberwell School of Arts and Crafts in 1974 and set up as a studio potter. I concentrated on making thrown, burnished and sawdust fired porcelain for many years. My current range of work includes planters, stools and birdbaths which were inspired by visits to India and Nepal. I use Craft Crank stoneware clay fired to 1260° C. Some pieces are finished with a blue ash glaze, others are textured green. My work is handbuilt by slabbing, press-moulding, free-hand modelling and using impressed decoration. I have exhibited widely in Britain and abroad, and I am on the Crafts Council Index of quality. A number of museums have bought my work for their collections, including Glasgow and Stoke on Trent. My plant towers are featured in Malcolm Hillier's book *Container Gardening*. Commissions include a pair of tree containers for the Ferens Art Gallery in Hull. Examples of my work were exhibited in The Potters Garden at Garden Festival Wales in 1992. I have written a book on *Sawdust Firing*, published 1994

John Higgins

JH

John Higgins My work is always handbuilt and constructed from a highly textured clay which may comprise of slab and thrown components. The forms are loosely based around the vessel and are informed by architecture and painting. The work requires the observer to move all around the forms to reveal changing surfaces, images and profiles. The surfaces incorporate dryness, texture and layers of colour. These layers of colioured surfaces are applied at different stages and fired to different temperatures using both reduction and oxidation firings up to and including 1120° C

Ashley Howard

Ashley Howard was born in Kent in 1963. After school he worked in a local graphics studio before studying ceramics at Medway College of Art and Design 1983-87. As a student he worked for potters John Pollex in Plymouth and Mike Goddard in the Dordogne. He also travelled to Northern India. He works for galleries and exhibitions using thrown, altered and handbuilt techniques at stoneware and earthenware temperatures.

Joanna Howells

Joanna Howells Born in 1960 Joanna's first career was in medicine - she took a B.A. in Medical Sciences at Cambridge University. However, in 1984 she decided to pursue, full-time, her love of ceramics. She went to the studio pottery course at Harrow College, from where she graduated with distinction. She exhibits widely in the UK and has exported her work to Europe and the USA.

Anita Hoy

Anita Hoy Mainly individual pieces, earthenware, stoneware, porcelain and some raku. Working alone. Trained at Copenhagen College of Art. Started and became head of studio departments at Bullers Ltd. Stoke-on-Trent, and Royal Doulton at Lambeth, working with porcelain and saltglazed stoneware. Looking for oneness of form and decoration, comprising carving, coloured slips and oxide brushwork, under or over clear and opaque coloured reduction fired glazes at 1260°C. Work illustrated in books and articles *(Doulton Lambeth Wares* by D Eyles 1976 and *Studio Porcelain* by Peter Lane 1980). Retrospective Bullers exhibition at Gladstone Pottery Museum 1978 and Doulton Story at Victoria and Albert Museum 1979. Represented with a collection at Victoria and Albert Museum and City Museum, Stoke-on-Trent. Taught for many years at West Surrey College of Art and Design. Work shown at the Crafts Council exhibition 'Influencial Europeans in British Crafts and Design' 1992.

John Huggins

John Huggins and his assistants make a wide range of frost-proof terracotta plant pots. Most are thrown, some are handpressed. Many of his pots are decorated with a motif of the life-giving forces - the sun and the rain. He also produces large green glazed press-moulded stoneware pots.

Anne James

Anne James The work is thrown in porcelain. Some forms are modified by beating. The pieces are covered with coloured slips and burnished with a spoon while still slightly damp. After biscuit firing they are decorated with layers of coloured slips and fired, often several times adding extra lustres, taken hot from kiln and smoked in sawdust. Ideas are drawn from many sources including the rich colours and surfaces of ethnic textiles and combined with the tactile quality of burnished clay. Work can be seen at Oxford Gallery, Montpellier, Stratford-on-Avon, Fenny Lodge, other galleries in UK and Gloucestershire Guild of Craftsmen.

John Jelfs

John Jelfs studied pottery at Cheltenham College of Art and set up present studio with wife Judy in 1973, making earthenware. Changed to stoneware in 1976. At present making a wide range of domestic ware and one-off pieces including some porcelain. Work sold through craft shops and galleries as well as from workshop.

Chris Jenkins

Chris Jenkins Born 1933. Trained as a sculptor and painter at Harrogate and the Slade School, finally as a potter at The Central School, London. I have been working with clay since 1957 in a variety of studios, currently in Marsden with a wood kiln in France. Essentially I produce a range of individual pieces fired to oxidised stoneware in an electric kiln, they are mostly decorated with slips using engraving and resist techniques. For some time I have been exploring the relationship between geometrical constructions and simple thrown forms, projecting two dimensional design on to three dimensional form.

Wendy Johnson

W

Wendy Johnson I studied at Derbyshire College of Higher Education (1988-90). All my work is handbuilt using, slab, pinch and modelling techniques. Inspiration is drawn from many sources including architecture, wildlife and floral images. Each piece of work is individually crafted using white earthenware clay and coloured with body stains and oxides. Work is then biscuit fired to prepare the surface for a final application of oxides and glazes. Colour is also inspired by nature, with deep blues, powdery greens, yellows and subtle pinks. My range includes clocks, candlesticks, vases, lidded boxes and various sized bowls and vessels.

Hazel Johnston

Hazel Johnston works in porcelain making thrown bottles and bowls. Clarity of form is very important and this together with subtly coloured and textured glaze surfaces are characteristic of her work. A dolomite glaze is used over various mixtures of metal oxides and a restrained use of gold lustre adds emphasis to some forms. All are fired in an 8 cu.ft. electric kiln. Trained at Manchester, N.D.D. 1st class Hons. A.T.D. Taught at Mid-Warwickshire College and produced her own work, slipware, followed by domestic stoneware, then porcelain in the last 14 years. The present studio was set up in 1977.

David Jones

David Jones Born 1953. I graduated from Warwick University in Philosophy and Literature exactly 20 years ago in 1974. Since then I have been a potter; for 15 of those years concentrating on work produced in, and inspired by, the raku technique. A lot of the objects made have been referential, not merely to the objects of the Japanese Tea-ceremony, but also to the European tradition of ritual tea drinking. I detect in this commenting-on a vestige of that philosophical training. 1993 Inax Prize winner. Currently senior lecturer (associate) at Wolverhampton University. Recent exhibitions in Britain, Malaysia, Japan, Belgium and Germany.

Walter Keeler

Walter Keeler Functional pottery of an individual nature in saltglazed stoneware.

Ruth King

Ruth King trained at Camberwell School of Arts and Craft from 1974-77 and established her own workshop in London in 1978. In 1981 she moved to York where she now lives and has her own studio. Her pots are handbuilt using various techniques of construction to produce individual decorated pieces in saltglaze stoneware. Ruth King has exhibited throughout Great Britain and has work in collections at the Victoria and Albert Museum, Castle Museum, Nottingham, Ulster Museum, Belfast, York City Art Gallery and Museum of Scotland, Edinburgh.

Gabriele Koch

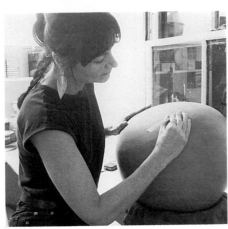

Gabriele Koch Degree in English, History, Political Science at Heidelberg University. Studies and travels in Spain inspired me to want to work with clay. 1979-81 Goldsmiths' College Diploma in Art & Design, Ceramics. 1982 Crafts Council Setting-up Grant. Since then my work has been exhibited widely in the UK and abroad and is housed in many private and public collections including the Sainsbury Collection, museums in Frankfurt, Karlsruhe, Lorrach and Zurich, art galleries in Leeds, Gateshead, Aberdeen, Aberystwyth Arts Centre and the European Investment Bank in Luxembourg. All pieces are handbuilt, burnished and subsequently smoke fired.

Anna Lambert

A4L
Anna Lambert.

Anna Lambert After graduating from Bath Academy of Art in 1980, I set up a workshop, first in Gloucestershire and since 1989 in Yorkshire. My work is all handbuilt earthenware. Methods of coiling, pinching and relief modelling are used to slowly build a variety of domestic forms - candlesticks, egg cups, jugs and large celebratory plates. These are painted with underglaze and lead glazes and reflect in colour and form land and seascape, the weather and seasons. I aim to combine function with evocative and observed images of country life to produce joyful individual pieces. I sell and exhibit my work throughout Britain and in Europe and USA, or by commission.

Peter Lane

P P

Peter Lane

Peter Lane is the author of *Studio Porcelain* (Pitman 1980), *Studio Ceramics* (Collins 1983), *Ceramic Form: Design and Decoration* (Collins 1988), *Contemporary Porcelain: Materials, Techniques and Expressions* (A&C Black 1994) and various articles on ceramics. He has exhibited widely and given numerous lectures and demonstrations in Europe, Australia, New Zealand, Canada and the USA. Most of his work is in porcelain (especially translucent bowls springing from narrow bases) carved, incised, inlaid, or painted with brightly coloured ceramic stains and glazes. Awarded the Silver Medal of the Society of Designer-Craftsmen in 1981. Represented in many public and private collections including the City Museum and Art Gallery, Stoke-on-Trent; City of Aberdeen Museum and Art Gallery; The Castle Museum, Norwich; The Royal Scottish Museum, Edinburgh; The National Gallery of Victoria, Melbourne, Australia; Utah Museum of Fine Arts, Salt Lake City, USA; etc.

David Leach

David Leach started in 1930 with father Bernard Leach, as a student, manager and partner at the Leach Pottery, St. Ives until 1956. Now after 64 years potting works alone on thrown stoneware and porcelain, mostly commissions, exhibitions and individual pots. Prices range from £5 to £500. Exhibits regularly in the United Kingdom, USA, Japan and the Continent in group or one-man shows. Work in many national and continental museums. Past chairman of the Craft Potters Association and council member of the Crafts Council. Late external assessor for studio pottery courses Harrow School of Art, Scottish Education Department and other colleges of art. Initiated Dartington Pottery Training Workshop 1975 with the late David Canter. Gold Medallist Istanbul 1967. One time Head Ceramics Department Loughborough College of Art 1953-54. Spends part of each year giving lectures, demonstrations, workshops chiefly in USA, Canada and on the Continent.

Janet Leach

Janet Leach was born in Texas, USA in 1918. Moved to New York to study sculpture. Began studying pottery in 1948. Met Bernard Leach, Shoji Hamada and Soetsu Yanagi when they toured America in 1952. Went to Japan to study under Hamada in 1954. In 1956 came to England to marry Bernard Leach and now runs the Leach Pottery in St. Ives, Cornwall making her own individual pots. Likes using several different clays and firing techniques - all reduction stoneware. Has held regular one-person exhibitions in England and Japan and her work included in many national and international shows and collections.

John Leach

MUCHELNEY

John Leach I established Muchelney Pottery, Somerset in 1964 with my wife Lizzie and family. Looking back over almost 35 years potting I feel indebted to my father and grandfather, to Ray Finch and Colin Pearson, who were instrumental in forming the ideas and themes of pottery which I still embrace. I did not have a formal art school training, but have grown out of a strong workshop tradition, disciplined in the production of functional pottery. Not until 1983 did I feel able to free myself from the limitations of this work ethic to produce signed individual work exploring a wider range of shapes and creative impulses. Examples of this work are always available in the pottery shop alongside our classic range of wood-fired kitchen stoneware. The pottery team consists of Lizzie and myself as partners. Nick Rees whose contribution to the repeat stoneware production and the day-to-day running of the pottery is vital, and our able student Ali Prince.

Eileen Lewenstein

Eileen Lewenstein makes individual pots and objects in stoneware and porcelain. The sea and its ability to both wear away through constant motion and yet also built up through barnacles and mussels provides a constant fascination and is her main source of inspiration. Recent work has included paired forms; thrown and altered porcelain and coiled stoneware. Exhibited widely in this country and abroad including Portugal 1990; Australia 1988; USA 1983, 1985; New Zealand 1983; Yugoslavia 1984, 1985 and Istanbul 1992. Represented in many public and private collections including Victoria and Albert Museum; Glasgow Art Gallery and Museum; Museum of Decorative Arts, Prague; Museum of Contemporary Ceramics, Bechyne, Czechoslovakia; Villeroy and Boch Sculpture Park, Mettlach, Germany; Auckland Institute and Hawkes Bay Art Gallery and Museum, New Zealand. Co-editor *Ceramic Review* Co-editor with Emmanuel Cooper *New Ceramics* Studio Vista 1974.

Laurence McGowan

Laurence McGowan Born Salisbury 1942. Set up own workshop in 1979 after earlier career making maps and interpreting aerial photos in various parts of the world. Trained at Alvingham and with Alan Caiger-Smith, Aldermaston. Traditional majolica decorative techniques employed on quiet, wheel-thrown functional forms. Various stain and oxide mixtures painted on zirconium opacified Cornish Stone based glazes. Electric fired to cone 9 (1260°C). Decorative motifs taken from plant and animal forms, applied to both enhance the pot's form and reflect something of the exuberance of nature. Interests relating to work include lettering/calligraphy and the decorative arts of the Islamic world.

Mal Magson

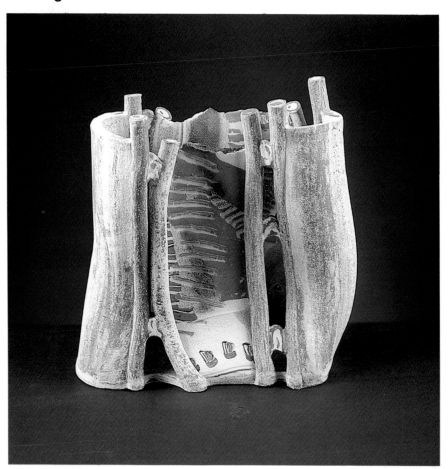

Mal Magson has explored techniques of staining and laminating clay for the past 22 years during which time her work has been exhibited and collected   throughout the UK and abroad. Present production is limited by teaching commitments at University College Scarborough, but recent work has involved experiments with a 'T' material/stoneware mix to create a vehicle for stained stoneware and porcelain inlay and additional drawn and impressed marks. Large clay slabs are the format for these experiments which often result in relief panels or robust and large-scale sculptural forms combining slabbed and extruded elements.

Jim Malone

Jim Malone Born 1946. High fired stoneware.

West Marshall

West Marshall studied pottery at Harrow School of Art and set up his first workshop in Norfolk in 1970. During the seventies he made reduced stoneware domestic ware and some slip decorated, one-off thrown pots. He now lives in Buckinghamshire and produces small quantities of enamel decorated porcelain domestic ware. He currently teaches on the Workshop Ceramics (BA Hons) course at the University of Westminster, Harrow.

Will Levi Marshall

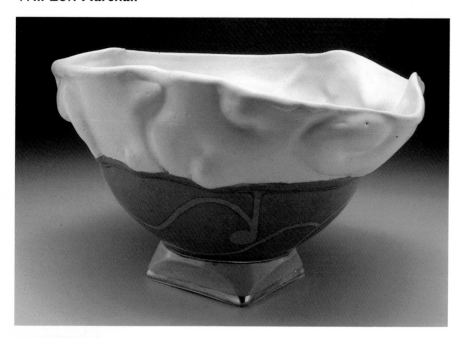

Will Levi Marshall There was a young potter from Dumfries/ Who needed psychological release/ So he made some pots/ With stripes and spots/ And it kept him out of trouble with the police.
Will Levi Marshall studied at Manchester Metropolitan University gaining a B.A. Hons in three dimensional design and then went on to complete a Master of Fine Arts (Ceramics) degree at Alfred University, New York, USA. He currently runs a pottery in the borders of Scotland, where he produces a range of functional domestic stoneware. Will's work is fired in an electric kiln to 1280°C with additional overglaze enamel and lustre firings.

Leo Francis Mattews

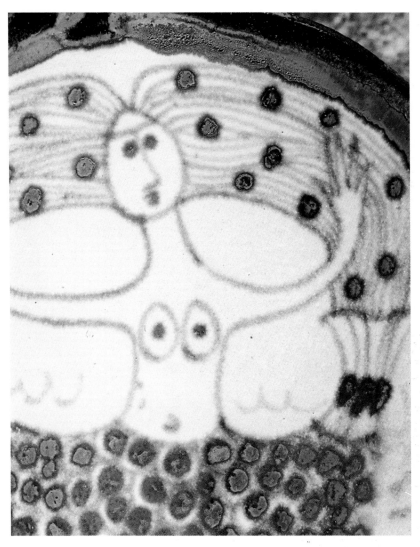

Leo Francis Matthews studied graphics at Manchester College of Art and ceramics at Stoke-on-Trent College of Art.   Lectured on ceramics for over twenty-four years at various major colleges of art in Britain. Produces sculptural ceramics, murals and some domestic studio pottery.

Marcio Mattos

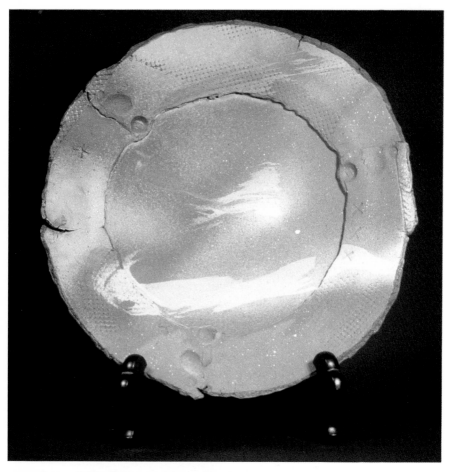

Marcio Mattos Trained initially as a musician and later in ceramics at Goldsmiths' College. Also participated in the International Ceramics Workshop, Tokoname, Japan. Has lectured and exhibited widely, with work in private and public collections in Britain, Holland, France, Lebanon, Brazil and Japan. Works in red stoneware and 'T' material, gas fired. Individual pieces are entirely handbuilt, with sprayed and brushed glazes. As in music, the creative process of free improvisation is important to work.

Peter Meanley

pm 94

Peter Meanley Since 1987 my output has been almost totally limited to the manufacture of individual teapots. All teapots are salt fired at cone 10 and capable of use. Ideas are based upon things seen, and my conscience, that of wanting to produce the very best and looking closely at fine historical examples (not necessarily teapots). Presently Senior Course Tutor: BA Hons. Fine Craft Design, University of Ulster at Belfast.

Eric James Mellon

Eric James Mellon

in foot ring : 1994 $\frac{n}{m}$ Ath used title

Eric James Mellon Born 1925. Studied Watford, Harrow and Central School of Arts & Crafts, London. Creates brush drawn decorated ceramic fired 1300°C, using tree and shrub ash glazes. Represented in the Victoria & Albert Museum and collections in Britain and internationally. 'Drawing on to clay is firing thoughts into ceramic. The concern is not academic correctness in drawing but to create work of visual decorative poetic surprise and aesthetic satisfaction'. Photograph (above) Vera Wardroper with a musician. Bowl 10.5 " diameter; philadelphus ash glaze. One of six pieces in the collection of Herta and Hansgorge Koch, Germany. See: Rogers P. *Ash Glazes* (Black/Chilton 1991) and 'Magic and Poetry' *Ceramic Review* No. 114, 1988.

Jon Middlemiss

Jon Middlemiss Making sculptural and vessel forms full time since 1979. Exhibitions in UK, Belgium, Germany, Holland, France, Italy and USA, including touring exhibitions, lectures, demonstrations. Awarded Gold Medal 13th Biennale, Vallauris 1992. Honourable Mentions at Mino Triennale, Zagreb Triennale with other awards in Germany and Belgium. Collections include Keramion, Kestner and Cologne Museums. Opening of Keramik-Studio-Middlemiss, Germany 1990. Member of Chambre-Syndicale des Ceramistes et Ateliers, and Crafts Council Index. 'A major influence has been the ceramics of the natives of Arizona which reflect a sense of order based on the foundations of a spiritual philosophy that sees even the harshest of life's experiences as meaningful and of consequence. Meditation offers me the same foundation."

David Miller

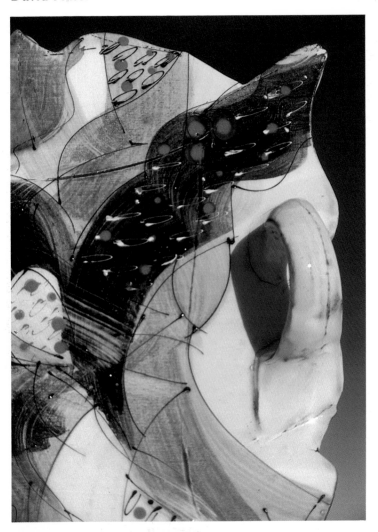

David Miller Born in London. Studied sculpture, printmaking and ceramics at Ravensbourne and Brighton Colleges of Art. Set up workshop in London in the 1970s. Now living and working in Southern France making one-off pieces and a range of highly decorated functional ware based on traditional French slipware. Exhibitions in France, Holland, England and Germany.

Ursula Mommens

Ursula Mommens 'I learnt for two years under William Staite Murray at the Royal College of Art and much later had the great good luck of working with Michael Cardew at Wenford Bridge. I started off converting an old cowhouse in Kent and after marriage to Julian Trevelyan worked at Durham Wharf, Hammersmith Terrace, London. I now work at the pottery I set up 37 years ago in South Heighton, Newhaven, making useful stoneware using mainly wood ash glazes on our own body - fired in Chris Lewis's big wood-fired kiln or my small gas one.

Aki Moriuchi

AKI MORIUCHI

Aki Moriuchi Born in Tokyo, Japan. Started pottery in various part-time pottery classes in London with a short period of training in Japan. Trained at Harrow College (Westminster University) 1988-90, and Middlesex University 1990-92. Working in North London. I produce texture-glazed ceramics, incorporating some gestural elements. Most of them are multi-glazed and multi-fired, with the use of sandblast technique. I also make Japanese tablewares; they are for everyday use and for special occasions. At present I work between these two elements, which balance well within me in many ways.

Emily Myers

Emily Myers has been working as a London based studio potter since 1989. Her stoneware is distinctive for its strong controlled thrown forms and intense barium glazes. She produces a range of vases, dishes and lidded pots to order, and also works for exhibitions. She is on the Crafts Council Selected Index and her work can be seen at the Guggenheim Museum shop in New York.

Susan Nemeth

Nemell

Susan Nemeth Born 1957. Bournville School of Art 1973-75; Wolverhampton Polytechnic B.A. (Hons) 1975-78. Maker of one-off handbuilt porcelain bowls, platters, vases, tiles, commemorative plaques, and specially commissioned tableware 10cm-45cm dia. 1280°C. The decoration is integral. Using many layers of stained porcelain slips and inlays, rolled and stretched, a high density of colour is achieved. Sanding between firings gives a smooth matt finish. Susan has exhibited widely in Europe, Japan and America, and has work in the collections of Inax Co.Ltd. Japan, Ulster Museum, University of Cardiff and the Leicestershire Collection for Schools. In 1990 she won the Inax Design Prize. She is on the Crafts Council Selected Index.

Colin Pearson

Colin Pearson Born London 1923. Studied painting at Goldsmiths' College. Makes individual pieces in porcelain and stoneware. Winner of the 33rd Grand Prix at Faenza, Italy, and in 1980 was awarded a major Crafts Council Bursary for study in the Far East. Has work in many public and private collections. Has done regular workshops and slide presentations in the UK, on the Continent, USA, Malaysia and Australia. A member of the International Academy of Ceramics, and on the Crafts Council Slide Index. Vice Chairman of London Potters.

Jane Perryman

Jane Perryman trained at Hornsey College of Art and later spent a year at Keramisch Werkcentrum in Holland. The pots are handbuilt, using coiling and sometimes press-moulding techniques, and inspired by African and Early Celtic pots. They are covered with coloured slips, burnished and bisque fired to 980°C, then treated with various forms of resist and fired in sawdust. I exhibit regularly both in England and abroad and my work is in private and public collections. Presently serving on the Council of the Craft Potters Association. My book *Smoke Fired Pottery* will be published by A & C Black in March 1995.

Richard Phethean

Richard Phethean trained at Camberwell, graduating in 1976, and in the studios of Colin Pearson and Janice Tchalenko making domestic stoneware. An interest in slip-decorated terracotta began with traditional tools and techniques, and evolved into a more personal style significantly influenced by a two-year period working in Papua New Guinea as a crafts project volunteer. Range of work includes the classic thrown vessel forms made as individual pieces and limited editions or commissions of tableware. His broad pottery teaching experience includes one-to-one tuition in throwing as a speciality. Author of *Throwing* in the 'Complete Potter' series and producer of a growing series of throwing video cassettes.

Peter Phillips

Peter Phillips works with his wife Julie making a variety of decorative and domestic pieces in stoneware and porcelain. These are fired in a 12 cu.ft. gas kiln to cone 9. He makes his own glazes which vary from matt to shiny, stained with oxides. Peter and Julie also have a studio in France (Dordogne). Peter hold s classes both in Kent and in the Dordogne.

John Pollex

John Pollex trained at Harrow College of Art and commenced his pottery career working for Bryan Newman and Colin Pearson. He set up his own workshop in 1971 and for many years produced traditional slip decorated ware. In the mid 1980s he felt the need for a change. He had long been influenced by American ceramics admiring their bright colours and improvised forms. He sees his work in the area of three dimensional painting whereby clay substitutes canvas.

Christine-Ann Richards

CAR

Christine-Ann Richards Trained at Harrow School of Art and Technology (1971-73) under Mick Casson. Worked for Bryan Newman and David Leach. Started own workshop within Barbican Arts Group (1975-83). I now live and work at home. The 1978 CPA trip to China had a radical effect on my work and way of life. Since then I have studied Chinese art, taken people to China and continued developing my own work. I produce thrown porcelain as well as large vitrified earthenware vessels suitable for interiors, conservatories and gardens. Some of these have incorporated water features. Work in public and private collections. Exhibits at home and abroad. I work alone.

David Roberts

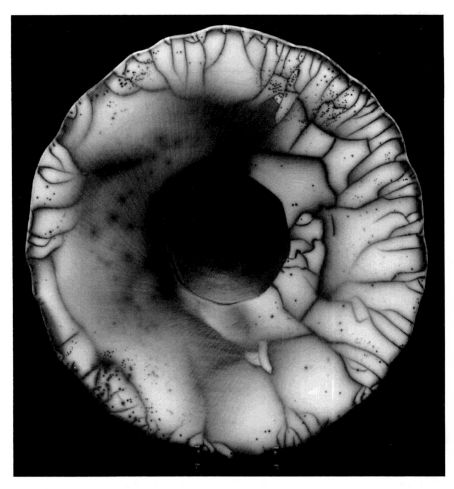

David Roberts Handbuilt raw fired vessels.

Jim Robison

Jim Robison produces a range of sculpture and functional work. Large scale, slabware, colourful ash glazes and rich surface details are recognised trademarks. The Yorkshire landscape, with its patterns of green fields and dry stone walls, is a primary source of inspiration. American born and trained, he moved to Holmfirth and established his present studio in 1975. He exhibits widely in the UK and abroad and has completed numerous commissions for architects and landscape designers. Current activities include special interests in architectural murals and garden sculpture.

Phil Rogers

Phil Rogers Born in Newport, South Wales in 1951. Came to live in Mid Wales in 1977 and moved to our present site in 1984. Most of my pots are thrown and then fired in either a 65 cu.ft. downdraught reduction kiln or saltglazed in a slightly smaller version of the same kiln. I make extensive use of wood ash and local rocks and clays for the glazes in both kilns. Our series of summer workshops continue in the converted stone barn which is the workshop overlooking the upper Wye Valley. I have exhibited in many galleries both in the UK and abroad and pots are held in a number of public and private collections, most notably the National Museum of Wales, Newport Museum and Art Gallery, University of Wales Collection, Aberystwyth, Bill Ismay Collection, Llantarnam Grange Handling Collection, Deggs Industrial Minerals Collection, Dyfed, and Gwent County Councils. Private collections particularly in USA and Japan. 1993 visited Ethiopia to begin a women's pottery project in Gondar and then, later in the same year, lectured and gave workshops in the USA. Member of the Crafts Council Selected Index of Makers and author of *Ash Glazes* (A&C Black 1991) and *Throwing Pots* (A&C Black 1994). Currently Chairman of the Craft Potters Association.

Duncan Ross

Duncan Ross established his present workshop near Farnham in 1989, after a period of study and exploration into terra sigillata techniques. Working with burnished earthenware he has developed a range of individual forms with which he aims to achieve a sense of balance, with surface patterns that repeat and move in curves and sweeping lines. These textures are built up using inlaid and resisted layers of sigillata. The work is fired several times and strongly smoked to create a range of colours from light orange to greens, greys and blacks.

Antonia Salmon

Antonia Salmon Born London 1959. Studied Geography at Sheffield University (1979-81) and Studio Pottery at Harrow School of Art (1981-83). Since 1985 I have worked on one-off and limited editions of burnished and smoke-fired vessels. These are all characterized by my interest in exploring the qualities of movement and stillness through form and space. Work is exhibited widely in Britain and on the Continent.

Patrick Sargent

Patrick Sargent studied wood firing and trained at Farnham (W.S.C.A.D.) under Paul Barron and Henry Hammond 1977-80. Established present workshop in the Emmental region of Switzerland in 1994. Woodfires a five cubic metre single chambered cross draught climbing kiln with demolition timber to 1320˚C. Firings lasting around 60 hours. Most work is thrown, using momentum wheels and clay is prepared by foot. A wide variety of thrown qualities are achieved more as a result of intensity and duration of the firing, the style of kiln packing and the desposit of ash than from a conscious attempt to formally decorate. Exhibits and demonstrates in the UK and Europe.

David Scott

D.S.

David Scott Born in Yorkshire, studied Stoke-on-Trent and Royal College of Art. Over recent years the work I have made has varied from the strictly functional at one extreme to periods of time exploring abstract non-functional themes. I am a full-time lecturer running a degree course in ceramics at Loughborough College of Art and Design, and this activity both constrains and stimulates my making, but allows me to pursue areas of the craft as they interest me with a measure of independence. Work in various public and private collections including the Victoria and Albert Museum.

Ray Silverman

Ray Silverman Trained at Camberwell School of Art and Crafts, London and University of London Goldsmiths' College. Chairman of London Potters, Fellow of the Society of Designer-Craftsmen. On the Crafts Council Index. Solus Exhibitions including Victoria and Albert Museum, London (Man Made Series). Exhibited widely in group exhibitions throughout the world. My work has ranged from thrown tableware, handbuilt pieces to working as a designer in the ceramic industry. Over the past 15 years I have devoted the time in my workshop to producing individual thrown forms in porcelain and stoneware.

Michael Skipwith

 s

Michael Skipwith Lotus Pottery was founded in 1957 by Michael and Elizabeth Skipwith who had first met as students at Leeds College of Art. From 1957-79 they ran the pottery employing up to 17, making green glazed domestic earthenware fired in electric kilns. In 1980 after converting part of their large old stone built farm Michael recommenced potting on his own using a wood-fired kiln which gives a rich toatsed colour to unglazed pots, particularly suited to garden pots. He also makes glazed kitchenware and more recently porcelain bowls and vases. He is the Devon stockist of Potclays range of clays and raw materials.

Peter Smith

Peter Smith Formerly a research chemist specialising in high temperature chemistry. Started Bojewyan Pottery in 1975. At present making both ceramics and sculpture.

John Solly

John Solly Born Maidstone, Kent 1928. Studied Maidstone, Camberwell and Central Schools of Art. Short working periods with Walter Cole at Rye Pottery, and Ray Finch at Winchcombe Pottery. Established own workshop in Maidstone 1953. Since 1960 has run a regular summer school at the pottery. 1986 moved to Peasmarsh. Still making slipware and high fired earthenware. A founder member of the Craft Potters Association. First Chairman of Kent Potters Association. Fellow Society of Designer-Craftsmen. Member Rye Society of Artists. 1983 invited to run slipware workshop, Middletown, CT, USA. 1989 slipware seminar, Bussum, Holland. 1993 visiting lecturer, La Trobe University, Bendigo, Australia.

Peter Stoodley

Peter Stoodley makes unglazed inlaid slip decorated planters, sometimes with applied strips, fired in an electric kiln. Studied painting at Bournemouth and Goldsmiths' Schools of Art. During Art Teachers Diploma chose pottery as craft subject at Camberwell. Returned to Bournemouth in 1951 and remained as lecturer until 1980. Set up first workshop in 1952 and began making plant pots to commission. Moved to Lymington in 1987 into larger workshop with additional gas fired kiln. Still makes planters to order or for exhibition but seeks to do more throwing and to return to using glazes on smaller handbuilt pots.

Harry Horlock Stringer

Harry Horlock Stringer One of the 1950s wave of 'Painter turned Potter' who had to teach themselves, he found a new way of understanding the formulation and making of glazes without resort to the use of molecular formulae. Always very interested in teaching, he built a school, literally with his bare hands. This was opened in 1965 and has catered for a large international summer school ever since. An interest in raku in the late fifties led to the first book on the subject to be written in the West in 1967, also designing and making an electric raku kiln safe enough to use in the classroom in 1965. Being confined to the use of electricity only, much research has gone into the development of quality in oxidising atmospheres, this led to the discovery of the first 'Reactive Slip' in 1975. Served for nine years on the Council of the Craft Potters Association during its formative years and was Editor of their journal for a number of years. He continues to contribute to potters' journals. In the fifties he had a workshop in the old Fulham Pottery making once-fired earthenware for domestic use later transferring to Taggs Yard where twice-fired earthenware was made. At present stoneware and a small amount of porcelain, mostly for domestic use is produced. Work has been exhibited in a number of different countries where it is in museums and private collections. He was head of an art department in a Teacher Training College for many years and lectures at home and abroad by invitation.

Helen Swain

Helen Swain At present making burnished earthenware. After studying painting, pottery and modelling, I worked with Harry and May Davis in Cornwall. Then three years at Royal Doulton (Lambeth) with Agnete Hoy, carving and painting saltglazed stoneeware. From 1963-93 I taught at Goldsmiths' College (London) in the fine ceramic department (now so short-sightedly closed). I had a solus exhibition at CPA in 1961 and have contributed to sixteen groups since then.

Sabina Teuteberg

Sabina Teuteberg has a fine-art background and trained in ceramics at Croydon College of Art and Design. Decorates mainly clay slabs with coloured clay inlays and slips. At present the colourful abstract patterned slabs are turned into a range of functional ceramics by the method of jigger and jolley. All work is high fired earthenware. Work has been exhibited and sold throughout the UK and abroad. Example of work in public collections: University of Wales, Cleveland Country Museum Service, Ulster Museum, Crafts Council Collection.

Owen Thorpe

Owen Thorpe studied at Willesden Art School (1951-56), Harrow School of Art (1959-61) and Bournemouth College of Art (1961-62). Set up workshop in Ealing, London 1970. Moved to Priestweston, Shropshire 1975, Churchstoke Powys 1981. Works alone. Produces a range of domestic stoneware pottery using coloured and locally occurring slips and wax-resist decoration. All work is wheel-thrown and is fired with electric oxidising firing. Also produces range of garden pottery decorated with coloured slip brushwork as well as highly decorated individual pieces using a technique like majolica but at stoneware temperatures. Tin glazes are employed, some tinted cream or light blue, with elaborate brushed patterns applied to the unfired glaze. Has exhibited widely.

Ruthanne Tudball

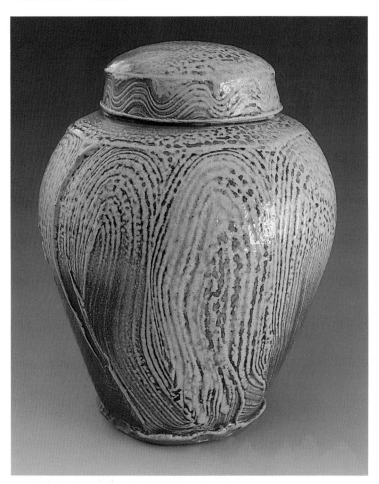

Ruthanne Tudball Born in California, USA. Post-graduate Diploma in Ceramics from Goldsmiths' College after years of being mainly self-taught and after gaining an honours degree in English and a Post-Graduate Certificate in Education. All my work is stoneware, raw glazed, slip decorated and once-fired soda-glazed with sodium compounds other than salt. My main concern is with the clay and the pleasure of manipulating it during throwing. I want to make forms that capture the soft plasticity of the material and have both dignity and a lively freshness. Soda glazing can have dramatic effects on the surfaces of the pots emphasizing the making process and path of the flames across the work, rendering each pot unique. I make my pots to be lived with, handled and used.

Tina Vlassopulos

Tina Vlassopulos Individual pieces in stoneware using coloured slips or burnished red earthenware.

Josie Walter

Watter .

Josie Walter Born 1951. Trained as an Anthropologist, then as a teacher, and finally as a Potter on the Studio Ceramics Course, Chesterfield College of Art 1976-79. Spent an invaluable six months as a repetition thrower with Suzie and Nigel Atkins, Poterie du Don, Auvergne, France. Shared a workshop with John Gibson for eight years and then moved to an old mill for the next eight. Over the past few years I have experimented with combinations of paper resist, colour infill and slip trailing (first cutting and then tearing the paper to give a softer effect) However, feeling that the images had become too static and dense, I have been exploring the qualities inherent in my materials. Pouring the slips thinly to create overlapping layers and to let the red earthenware body show through. Using the marks of the brush, highlighted with sgraffito, has created a greater sense of movement and a fresh perspective. All the work is once fired and to cone 03.

John Ward

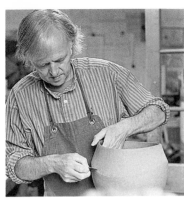

John Ward Born in London 1938. Studied ceramics at Camberwell School of Arts and Crafts (1966-70). Set up first workroom in 1970 and taught part-time at an adult education institute until 1979 before moving to Wales to pot full-time. Central theme is simple hollow forms, often derived from the bowl. Pots are fired in an electric kiln - biscuit fired to 1000°C, glaze 1250°C. Matt glazes are applied by spraying, pouring and painting; black, white and blue/green being most frequently used but experiements are in progress to introduce more colour.

Sasha Wardell

Sasha Wardell Born 1956 in Sri Lanka. Studied ceramics at Bath Academy of Art (1976-79). North Staffordshire Polytechnic (1979-81) and Ecole Nationale d'Art Decoratifs in Limoges, France. Has taught in various art colleges since 1981 and set up workshop, exhibiting mainly in the UK and abroad since 1982. Moved to France in 1989 and re-established workshop near Brive-la-Gaillarde where now running summer courses in plaster work and slip-casting. Materials and processes involve slip- casting bone china to an egg-shell thinness to enhance translucency. Models are produced by plaster-forming techniques using a turning lathe and hand-carving. After moulding, the pieces are fired three times. This includes a soft-firing, after which the work is sanded, a 1260°C firing to mature the body, and finally, a 1080°C firing to harden on the decoration, which is airbrushed through a series of intricate masks.

John Wheeldon

John Wheeldon Born 1950. Trained at Chesterfield College of Art and Wolverhampton Polytechnic 1969-74. My work is thrown mainly from a black stoneware body and decorated with precious metal lustres, applied by using stamps or, increasingly, by brushing over latex resist trailing. In contrast to this I am becoming more involved in raku, enjoying it for its directness and lack of control. I sell through shops and galleries throughout Britain and Europe and have work in public and private collections. Presently I am potter-in-residence at Repton School and a Council Member of the CPA. My work is illustrated in several publications including *Pottery Decoration* by John Gibson, *Lustres* by Margery Clinton and *Pottery, a Manual of Techniques* by Doug Wensley

David White

David White My work is predominantly crackle glazed porcelain. I have produced a wide range of glazes which craze in various ways. The glazes are then blended by carefully controlled spraying, using up to five glazes on a pot. On cooling the pots are coated with a carbon based ink and washed off immediately. By doing perpetual tests and experiments and copious notes of how the pots were glazed, a degree of control on the crazing can be achieved. Almost 50% out of each firing are considered unsatisfactory and are reglazed and refired.

Mary White

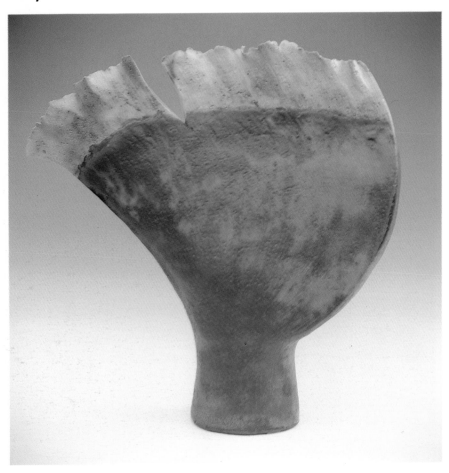

Mary White Trained at Newport School of Art, Hammersith School of Art and Goldsmiths' College. Initiated the Ceramic Workshop in Atlantic College 1962-72, then set up own workshop. With my husband Charles, moved into wine-producing village in S.W. Germany in 1980 to be in the middle of Europe. Was awarded the Staatspreis fur Rheinland-Pfalz for Ceramic in 1982, then other prizes internationally. I have exhibited all over Europe and USA and was proud to have work shown in the Musee des Arts Decoratifs, Louvre, Paris. My work is in many international collections and museums and is represented in numerous international books, magazines and catalogues. My newest work uses coloured inlays (porcelain). I am also a calligrapher and sometimes integrate letters in clay forms. I want time to enjoy my wonderful surroundings, so I am now limiting my output.

Caroline Whyman

Caroline Whyman went to art school with the intention of becoming a painter and became fascinated by clay and so went on the study ceramics at Camberwell School of Art. Since then she has had four pottery workshops in London. She began by making stoneware but gradually moved to porcelain because it enhanced the colours of her glazes. After visit to Japan, inspired by the textiles, she began to use decoration, and after a further trip to India the decoration grew to include precious metal lustres. The latest group of work shows a reduction of the surface pattern which has been refined to strong, bold statements using circles, triangles, squares, and grid patterns (re-occurring themes) which are enriched by the use of gold lustres and inlaid textured slips; combined with glazes of intense blue and turquoise.

David Winkley

David Winkley Born 1939. Originally trained as a painter at the School of Fine Art, Reading University and Pembroke College, Cambridge. After a brief period in Bristol, he moved in 1966 to West Somerset where he now makes an exceptionally wide range of stoneware pots for everyday use together with individual pieces in stoneware and porcelain. Firings are in a 230 cu.ft. two-chamber oil-fired kiln.

Mollie Winterburn

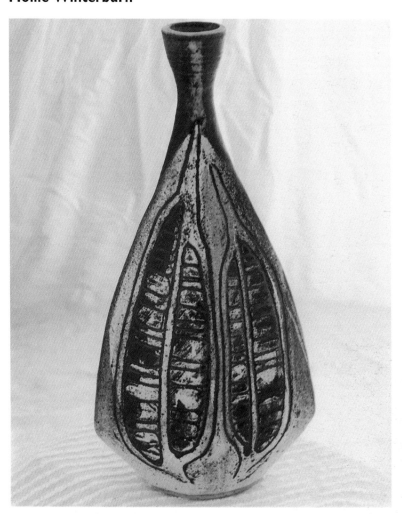

Mollie Winterburn All my work consists of individual pieces. I have heads, walls, journeys, crosses, candlesticks, houses, and many others. I keep a constant accumulation of bottles. I am happy working in this beautiful and lovely place.

Mary Wondrausch

Mary Wondrausch I work in earthenware using a honey glaze for the the more traditional slip-trailed pots. I specialize in individually commissioned commemorative plates, which customers are able to collect from the workshop, converted from an eighteenth century stable in a magical setting. These can also be posted worldwide. The subject of my gouache paintings is often reflected in the central decoration of the large cheese platters (see illustration). Latterly I have been developing a more painterly style with sgraffito fish and bird motifs using painted slips as well as oxides. My work is predominately functional, rather than sculptural.

Steve Woodhead

Steve Woodhead Born in Yorkshire, I trained as a biologist before moving into ceramics. I set up my studio at home in 1987. I work primarily in reduced stoneware making individual pieces, many based on traditional Korean forms. The central theme of my decoration is flowers of many shapes, flowing freely and wildly over the surfaces. Recently I have introduced a range of new colours to the flowers which has added a new dimension to the decoration, allowing me to more fully explore the theme of the English Country Garden.

Rosemary Wren and Peter Crotty

Rosemary Wren and Peter Crotty have for many years made animals and birds, using traditional handbuilding with patterns in stoneware glazes. On coming to the dramatic Scottish Highlands in 1990, Rosemary found ways to construct free-standing landscapes in stoneware and porcelain, again seeking for basic characteristics not only of pattern but also of light. The present economic climate being unfavourable to costly one-off pieces, the landscapes have developed into repeatable press-moulded hanging tiles. Stoneware glazes, velvet matts and lustres continue to enrich the basic incising. Rosemary's interest in making architectural drawings has enabled buildings and townscapes to creep in too, even from photographs. Enquiries invited. Founded in 1920, the Oxshott Pottery lives on.

Takeshi Yasuda

Takeshi Yasuda was trained at Daisei Pottery in Mashiko, Japan (1963-65). Worked in UK since 1973. Exhibits widely. Currently Associate Professor of Applied Art at University of Ulster in Belfast.

Joanna and Andrew Young

A & J YOUNG GRESHAM

Joanna and Andrew Young Dip. A.D. Ceramics at W.S.C.A.D. Farnham, Surrey, 1970-73. Worked in France with Gwyn Hanssen for six months, A.T.C. Goldsmiths' College, London 1974. Set up workshop 1975 in Hunworth, North Norfolk. Interest was, and still is, to provide interesting and practical everyday pots in a repeated range. Most pots are wheel thrown, some are shaped later by cutting and squaring in various ways. The main glaze is thinly applied, and once fired under reduction in a 100 cu.ft. gas kiln. The finish is often mistaken for saltglaze. 1981, moved to large workshop at Lower Gresham, Norfolk. Continued production with two assistants. The pots are sold to some shops and also through own shop next door to workshop. Occasional exhibitions, Crafts Council Bursary 1988.

Illustrated Directory of CPA Professional Members

A full list of Professional Members, together with their addresses, can be found on page 250

Billy Adams

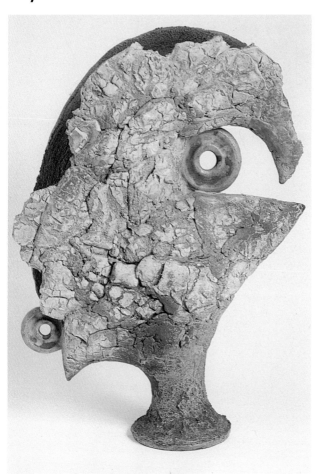

Billy Adams I am essentially an Irish potter, now living and working in Wales. My pots are handbuilt, usually from a thrown base, working upwards in several stages. Three different sorts of clay are used - an interior layer of 'craft crank', an intermediate layer of clay mixed to prevent shrinkage of the pot during firing, and an outer surface of porcelain which is encouraged to buckle and crack as I shape the form from inside the pot. This retains a fine hard texture, rather than becoming friable. At the midway stage I introduce a stylistically intrusive form such as a regular circular thrown handle or a smoothed rim - to represent the intervention of humans in the natural world.

Marilyn Andreetti

Marilyn Andreetti I trained at Farnham School of Art 1966-69, and taught art and design for ten years before deciding to work at home. I now work from a small converted coach house which overlooks my garden. I make some domestic stoneware and a few individual architectural pieces, but most of my current work is plates and dishes; thrown or press moulded in red clay. I decorate with underglaze colours and oxides on a cream coloured background and finish with sgraffito. I fire bisque to 1000°C and gloss to 1125°C in an electric kiln. I enjoy making colourful, decorative, commemorative yet functional ware. I sell through exhibitions, craft fairs and from the workshop.

Elizabeth Aylmer

Elizabeth Aylmer I regard myself as self-taught but in fact was generously instructed by a friend who had not only been to art college but also served a rigorous apprenticeship at Denby with the original classical throwers, thus for many years speed and precision were my goals. This was a good discipline and enabled me to produce large quantities of ware at reasonable prices. Having been raised in Zimbabwe my influences are drawn from African culture and this is instantly recognisable both in my domestic ware and the individual pots that I make when time allows.

Sylph Baier

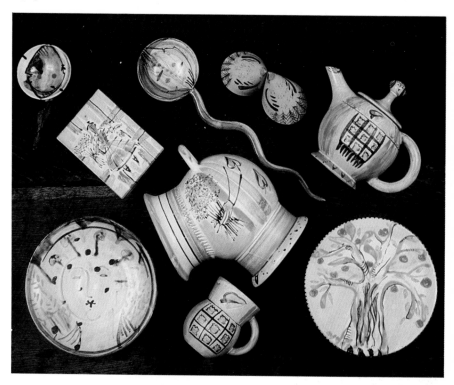

Sylph Baier Trained in Germany and West Wales. Attended Dyfed College of Art 1981-84 and is currently working in Brighton as part of a mixed -disciplined group studio. Produces various ranges of domestic ware using slips, sgraffito and majolica techniques.

Chris Barnes

Chris Barnes Born in Basingstoke in 1959. Studied sculpture at Goldsmiths' College and St. Martin's School of Art from 1978-82. Discovered ceramics at Islington Adult Education Institute and has been working with clay since 1987. He now shares a workshop with Keith Ashley at Farleigh Studios, Stoke Newington. The distinctive design and decoration of his reduced stoneware is shaped by diverse influences: an empathy for the nature of the making process itself and the generosity and breadth of treatment felt in certain peasant wares is given contemporary sensibilty in his functional pots.

Richard Baxter

Richard Baxter Born 1959. Studied ceramics at Loughborough College of Art finishing in 1981. Established first workshop with Crafts Council setting up grant. Most of my output is domestic earthenware - bold forms simply decorated. I fire to 1100°C in an electric top loading kiln. My one-offs explore ideas incompatible with domestic ware. They are sculptures that question the function, the relationship between inner and outer space, time/ageing processes and the point where the 'making' stops. Archaeological finds, primitive architecture, nature and geometry all contribute to the forms alongside marks developed from the making process - throwing, stretching, compressing, breaking.

John Bedding

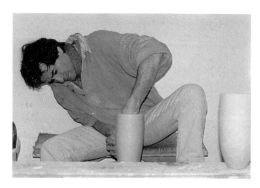

John Bedding Worked throughout the seventies at the Leach Pottery, interrupted by a year in France. In 1979 was invited by Shigeyoshi Ichino to study at his family's pottery in Tampa, Japan. Set up his own workshop in 1982 and now makes raku-fired individual pieces. They are wheel-thrown with burnished and textured surfaces. Some have silver nitrate and copper glaze decor, others are fumed with metallic salts. He exhibits widely and a full range of his work can be seen in the St. Ives Pottery Gallery which adjoins his workshop in the centre of St. Ives.

Julian Bellmont

Julian Bellmont opened the High Street Pottery in November 1993 after spending 13 years at the Aldermaston Pottery. He believes that pots should enhance everyday life so his pots are colourful and lustrous and should give the user a happy feeling when using them. The pots are made of a fine stoneware so they are practical, durable and aesthetic. In the showroom there is a good range of domestic ware and decorative ware. Commissions are also undertaken to individual requirements.

Kochevet Ben-David

K. Ben David .

Kochevet Ben-David My deep passion for functional domestic ware was awaked at Harrow College on the HND Ceramic Design course. I had intended to return to Israel, however, at the end of the course I set up a workshop and made London my home. I have been concentrating on designing and making functional and decorative domestic ware ever since, aiming to make delightful as well as durable pots. I work with Limoges Porcelain which provides a resonant background for the brushed and trailed coloured slip decorations. My decorative motifs are based upon the fruits and flowers of my homeland, my designs inspired by Art Deco.

Suzanne Bergne

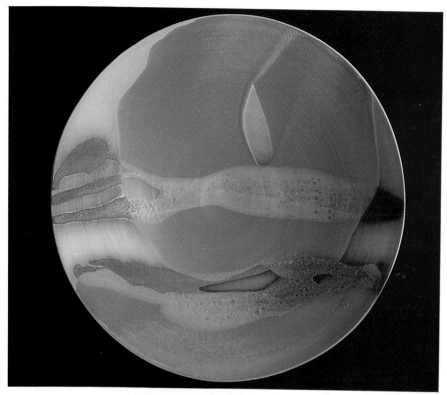

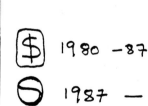

$ 1980 -87

⊖ 1987 —

Suzanne Bergne Born in Upper Silesia, studied literature and philosophy at Munich and Vienna Universities (1958-63). She travelled and worked for 20 years mainly in the Middle East. 1977-80 she trained formally as a potter at Croydon School of Art and Design, followed by seven years working and teaching in Athens and Hongkong. Finally, in 1987, she settled in London with a studio in Gloucestershire. She makes porcelain bowls and containers on the wheel and uses them as the canvas for coloured glazefields juxtaposed by various pouring methods. Recently she developed a way of altering the exactly thrown forms so that the dynamics of throwing and glaze pouring are emphasized. Hand in hand with an interest in watercolour technique and life drawing, glaze effects are developed that capture the soft edge quality of the first and the rhythm and volume contemplated in the latter. She sells on a regular basis through shops and galleries in UK, Germany and Japan. Her work is represented in the Victoria and Albert Museum, Hongkong Museum of Art and the Hongkong Tea Museum.

David Brown

David Brown For many years I have combined teaching with making and selling my own pots, and feel that the two activities provide the vital spark for each other. I have exhibited widely, including in America, where I twice participated on the teacher exchange programme. I have an unswerving obsession with the teapot. The duality of function and aesthetic, allied to the potential for sculptural fantasy continues to present the challenge. I am interested in organic growth and decay, fragmentation, reconstruction and the relationship between organic form and machinery. My pots naturally reflect these current concerns.

Jenny Browne

Jenny Browne My work is thrown stoneware and I enjoy working with strongly coloured slips. The decoration is done at the leather-hard stage using sgraffito, carving and painting. This way I can achieve bold, hard-edged designs. My glazes are clear or white, shiny or matt, sometimes enhanced with lustre. I have recently visited New Zealand where I was born and exhibited my work there.

Susan Bruce

Susan Bruce Studied ceramics at Cheltenham and at Lowestoft Colleges of Art. She taught art and ceramics in schools and FE colleges for a number of years full-time, now she teaches part-time, and is able to devote more time to ceramics. The work is handbuilt porcelain and T material with coloured slips painted on to the surface. The only glaze is on the inside of the jugs. Firing is to 1260°C in an electric kiln. Susan's work is currently exploring jugs, they are no longer functional, but seem to have a zany character of their own - almost as if they were conversing with the others in the group. She also makes large dishes, which have exuberant designs on a textured surface.

Karen Bunting

Karen Bunting I live and work in East London producing domestic ceramics. Mostly I like to make jugs, bowls and platters. These are usually thrown initially. They are then worked upon and decorated by incising or painting with oxides, often drawing upon geometrical patterning. I exhibit and sell work throughout the UK and abroad.

Jan Bunyan

Jan Bunyan I came to pottery late after taking a degree in French and working in various jobs for twelve years. Largely self-taught, I work in red earthenware, attracted by its warmth of colour and comfortable feel. My work is mostly thrown and decorated with underglaze colours applied by brush and sponge to a white background. It is clear-glazed and fired to 1100°C in an electric kiln. I have always wanted to make pottery for daily domestic use and hope that my pots give pleasure right through to the end of the washing-up.

Kyra Cane

Kyra Cane

Kyra Cane was born in 1962 in Southwell, Nottinghamshire and studied ceramics at Camberwell School of Art between 1982 and 1985. She received a Crafts Council Grant in 1987 and has exhibited widely since then. Her time is divided between her workshop in Mansfield and teaching at various colleges. She is principal member of the course team on the BA Hons Degree in Ceramics at Harrow, University of Westminster, London. Pots are all thrown on a wheel using stoneware clay and fired to 1285°C; lightly reduced in a gas kiln. Bowls and jugs are recurrent themes, working in series she is constantly engaged by the subtle variations between each piece. Layers of oxide, stain and glaze are applied to forms, which regain with firing something of the soft silky luscious experience of wet clay.

Tony Carter

Tony Carter
ENGLAND
©

Tony Carter stuudied ceramics at Bath Academy of Art 1971-74 (BA Hons) with post graduate year at Goldsmiths' College ATD. Started his own pottery with his wife Anita in 1978, specializing in slip cast work. Today the pottery has gained an international reputation for the collectable teapots made at the premises. Approximately 75% of its production is shipped worldwide. The pottery is based in the beautiful village of Debenham, set in the heart of Suffolk which is open to the public all year round, firsts and bargains available in the shop.

Trevor Chaplin

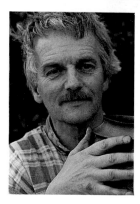

Trevor Chaplin I trained in pottery and design in the early 1970s then taught for 17 years, during this time I did my pottery part-time. I have been a full-time potter for the past six years, my studio is at my home in the depths of the Wiltshire countryside. All my pottery is high fired reduction stoneware, ash glazes are extensively used. I am particularly interested in altering basic thrown forms by manipulation, faceting, cutting and folding, etc. Most of my pots are extensions of the natural world around me in colours, shapes and forms; although there are strong traditional links. I am at present exploring soda glazing in my recently built 27 cu.ft. vapour kiln creating new territory to explore.

Ian Chapman

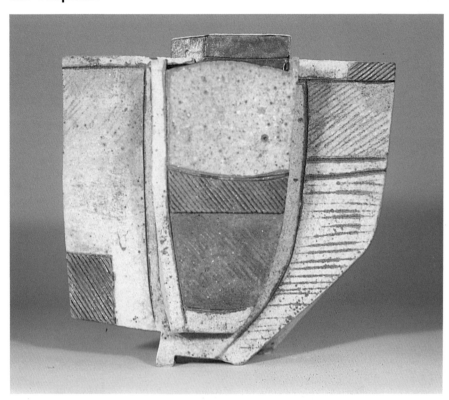

Ian Chapman uses slabs to make non-functional forms, wall panels or dishes, and boxes. His work is reduced stoneware fired in a gas kiln after being decorated with slips, oxides and matt glazes. They then sometimes receive further firings to enhance colour and textural balances. His ideas for forms and decoration are inspired by an interest in textured and formally altered arrangements of natural surfaces. The pots explore the relationship between form and surface treatment by aiming to balance the natural, in ceramic terms, with the formal design of lines, colours and textures imposed by the maker himself.

Desmond Clover

Desmond Clover My pots are thrown, some changed by cutting and adding rims and handles. I use a combination of abstracted and representational images and create depth within the surface of the vessel. I decorate with coloured glazes I have developed over the years. I like to build up the design like a painting, brushing, dipping and using wax resist, keeping it as fresh as possible. They are fired to 1280°C in a reduction atmosphere. I produce a variety of tableware but concentrate mainly on individual pieces. All my work is decorated with unique designs in stoneware and porcelain.

Rosemary Cochrane

Rosemary Cochrane Trained at Manchester Polytechnic. I live on a hillside in the Brecon Beacons National Park with my workshop in the barn adjacent to the old farmhouse. I produce saltglazed stoneware pots which are both practical and individual. Most are thrown on the wheel, the forms influenced by tradition and simple function. Rich and varied surface qualities are a feature of the saltglazed process and I use different clays, slips and oxides to give a range of colours. Currently I fire in a 30 cu.ft. catenary arch kiln. I sell my work through exhibitions and craft galleries.

Jo Connell

JC

Jo Connell Since leaving North Staffordshire Polytechnic in 1972 I have combined teaching with running a workshop. I have always been drawn to the colour and texture of clays rather than glazes, and enjoy the crispness of unglazed surfaces. I use slabs inlaid with coloured clays to make vessels and bowls, combining pressing, throwing and handbuilding. My influences range from rock strata, architecture and landscape to fabric and wallpaper - the pots themselves have a textile-like surface quality. Since moving to Witherley, a site of Roman occupation and pottery production, I have been inspired to make Roman-style mixing bowls as made here in the first century

Molly Curley

Molly Curley trained as an illustrator, but taught art and ceramics before potting full-time in 1982. She specialises in slip decoration on both earthenware and stoneware, exploring the techniques of trailing, feathering, sgraffito and currently sponging and pouring. Earlier-learned calligraphic skills have led to inscribed commemorative ware, mainly plates. Work includes a wide range of domestic ware, one-off jugs and bowls for exhibitions, in various bright and more muted colours. All work is thrown and fired by electricity in her workshop at her home. Founder member of the Makers Guild in Wales.

Louise Darby

Louise Darby Born 1957. Studied three dimensional design, specializing in ceramics at Loughborough 1975-78. Worked at Torquil Pottery, Henley-in-Arden 1978-83. Taught part-time ceramics 1981-90. 1984 set up own workshop in converted pigsty near Stratford-on-Avon. Works alone making finely thrown stoneware and porcelain ceramic pieces, often involving additional building and/or incising. Details and tactile qualities are as important as the form, line and texture created. Uses various clay mixtures with own glazes and fires in a ceramic fibre gas kiln to 1280°C. Louise exhibits and sells widely in Britain.

Joyce Davison

JD

Joyce Davison I established the pottery in Castle Acre in Norfolk seven years ago. All my work is thrown in stoneware or porcelain. Surface decoration is an important part of the finished work and various techniques are used to achieve this. Among these, brush painting, carving and incising feature prominently but others rely on a simple celadon or crackle glaze with sometimes a burnished metallic rim to add emphasis and enhance the shape of the form.

Nick Douglas

Nick Douglas studied at Plymouth College of Art and Design. He first worked as resident potter at Bickleigh Mill Craft Centre near Tiverton in Devon, then with John Stuart in Exeter and later at West Pottery and in his own workshop in Ivybridge. Nick spent two years (1987-88) in Nigeria based at the Minna Ceramics Centre, where he encouraged trainees towards self-supporting pottery production of domestic stoneware fired in wood and gas fired kilns. Nick secured a grant from the Canadian Development Commission to build and equip a studio pottery, which now runs successfully under the direction of Danlami Aliyu, a gifted Nigerian potter. Only two small gas injectors to fire the stoneware kiln needed to be imported. All the quipment, including two treadle operated kick wheels, raw material screens and the kiln were built by Danlami Aliyu. Nick returned to Devon and has now re-established his pottery, producing a range of domestic stoneware and some one-off pieces. Although his work may not appear to be influenced by his experience in Nigeria, he does claim to be producing pots with a maturity of form not previously evident. His use of a kick wheel similar in design to those in Nigeria, and the use of ash in most of his glazes have had their effect.

Bridget Drakeford

Bridget Drakeford

Bridget Drakeford works alone making individual thrown porcelain. Simple classical shapes glazed with a copper crackle glaze and touches of gold lustre. Now works from home in Herefordshire and will be experimenting with other firing technioques - raku and reduction firings. Established since 1977, and exhibits widely in the UK and abroad.

Victoria and Michael Eden

EDEN

Victoria and Michael Eden Since 1981 we have worked together making slip decorated domestic earthenware. We search to express the traditional qualities of slipware; liveliness, fluidity and often humour and add to these something of ourselves and the time we live in, with wood firing bringing new qualities to some of the work.

Kirsti Buhler Fattorini

Kirsti Buhler Fattorini I was born in Winterthur, Switzerland being fortunate to be brought up in a community where the visual arts were highly regarded. On completing my formal education I went to Rome to study painting and ceramics. I made handbuilt earthenware pots decorated with bright abstract designs. On marrying and moving to England I was unable to find the materials I was used to and changed to stoneware thrown pots which I continue to decorate with abstract designs. More recently I have included slipcast stoneware dishes suitable for domestic use. I particularly enjoy decorating and experimenting with glazes. Currently my designs are drawn from nature - animals, birds, fish and flowers.

Judith Fisher

JF

Judith Fisher Individual small-scale porcelain bowls and vases by the raku method in which the pot is withdrawn from a red-hot kiln and plunged into sawdust or other organic matter. When the surface has been coated with powdered copper unpredictable effects and colours, from purple to pink and turquoise, emerge. On other pieces the white surface receives interesting marks and veining from being fumed in stable sweepings.

Susan Ford

Susan Ford studied Fine Art and Ceramics at Exeter College of Art and Design where she obtained her B.A. Hons in Fine Art. She has been making ceramic sculpture since 1990. Her work is mostly figurative and the vitality and movement in her animal sculptures especially her dancing hares is much admired. Most of Susan Ford's work is bought by private collectors and displayed in private gardens. Her work includes some large commissions for public settings. Her sculptures are designed primarily for outside and are high fired and frost proof. Susan is very interested in architectural sculpture/ceramics.

Geraldine Fox

Geraldine Fox I studied ceramics at Wolverampton University. My work is handbuilt stoneware, and is influenced by such intricate structures as corals and wasp nests. I have exhibited locally, also in France and New Zealand.

Liz Gale

Liz Gale Trained as a teacher, specialising in textile arts, she taught in infant schools for ten years. Self-taught as a potter, she divided her time between teaching and ceramics, becoming a full-time potter in 1988 and moving to her first purpose-built workshop and showroom in 1992. Specialising in domestic reduction stoneware, she uses a combination of latex, sponging, trailing and wax resist, to create decoration reminiscent of textile designs. She constructed her 30 cu.ft. dry-built kiln which is propane fired. Since 1988 she has been involved in promoting the activities of Professional and Associate Members of the Craft Potters Association, being elected to the Council in 1992 when she became Honorary Secretary. Liz accepts commissions for dinner and tea services and individual decorative pieces.

Philip Gardiner

PG

Philip Gardiner After my initial training at North Staffordshire Polytechnic, I worked at several small potteries, including eight years as a production thrower, before setting up my own pottery in 1983. My work is all hand-thrown stoneware twice fired in an electric kiln. I make a very wide range of shapes, covering both functional and decorative items, decorated with incised work, sprigging and handmade whales. Most of my glazes contain zircon giving a range of pastel colours, the main exception being black.

Rodney George

Rodney George took up pottery six years ago at the age of 57 and in January 1992 he was accepted as a professional member of the Craft Potters Association. He works mostly with white earthenware clay and decorates on to the leatherhard. His themes are typically from nature - flowers, birds, fruit, etc. In the course of travelling widely throughout Europe, Africa and North America, he has met and been influenced by many of today's leading exponents of the craft. With the virtually unlimited scope that exists - the many clays, the glazes, the methods of decoration, the firing systems and perhaps, above all, the forming and shaping of the clay itself - he sees pottery as a wonderful vehicle where the possibilities and challenges are endlessly exciting and rewarding.

Graham Glynn

G Ɔ   on thrown ware

G.P.GLYNN   on handbuilt ware

Graham Glynn Studied at Oldham and Rochdale Schools of Art and at Wolverhampton Polytechnic. In 1981, after teaching for five years, set up a workshop in Skipton. In 1988 moved to Anglesey. Has moved yet again to new workshop in Sedberg, Cumbria. The workshop is open throughout the year. I work in oxidised stoneware in two main areas. Thrown ware in which I try to contrast precision of form with quite freely poured glazes of painted slips. Handbuilt figures, varying from 25cm up to lifesize. These are mainly silly old men or animal/human figures.

Paul Green

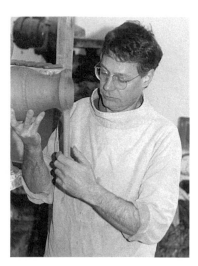

Paul Green established his present workshop, Abbey Pottery in Cerne Abbas, Dorset in 1986. He is largely self-taught, but completed a workshop training course at Chester School of Art after following a career in historic building conservation. He set up his first workshop in Wensleydale in the Yorkshire Dales, which he ran for six years. Abbey Pottery is a small country workshop producing a wide range of oven and tableware together with some more decorative porcelain. Most of the work is wheel-thrown and fired in a propane gas kiln to 1280°C in a reducing atmosphere. Glazes used are mainly ash, tenmoku, celadon and cobalt blue. The village of Cerne Abbas lies in beautiful countryside 8 miles north of Dorchester, the county town of Dorset. There is a well-stocked showroom at the pottery which is open throughout the year and is situated close to the famous Cerne Giant, a chalk figure carved into the nearby hillside.

Mark Griffiths

Mark Griffiths After ten years of making terracotta garden pots at my present workshop in Shropshire, I returned two years ago to high fired stoneware and the rekindling of a passion that started with my apprenticeship in 1973. Those years of disciplined production throwing now allow me the freedom to pursue new ideas and methods of making. My interest in using local materials with their variations in both slips and glazes are a continuing source of pleasure. A range of pots can be seen in the showroom.

Dimitra Grivellis

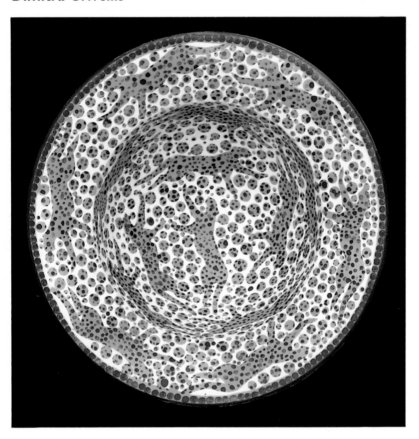

Dimitra Grivellis studied ceramics at Hammersmith School of Art and then gained wide experience as a production thrower at established potteries. Since 1984 Dimitra has been working exclusively in porcelain, producing individual pieces, developing and using sandblasting techniques to decorate them. Her work consists of bowls, vases, jars and plates. All are thrown using David Leach porcelain and oxidised to 1230/1260°C. Each piece is sandblasted, using a variety of resist masking materials, and colourfully decorated, mainly in relief. The decoration is inspired by wild animals and their habitats combined with traditional patterns from the relevant local culture. It is this combination that she loves, the beauty of porcelain, the controlled power of sandblasting, the joy of colour and a theme full of creative possibilities.

Morgen Hall

Morgen Hall makes a wide range of domestic tableware, often inspired by the food the work is intended for, from double egg cup and toast soldier sets, cake plates and tea cabarets to marshmallow jars with toasting forks. Most of the work is wheel thrown, but with the emphasis on the turning and finishing. A range of press-moulded work with low relief decoration called 'Mardubi Ware' is also made, along with some slab-built pieces such as tea trays. All the work is made from tin glazed red earthenware, and, although it is highly decorated, it is intended for everyday use.

Janet Halligan

JH94

Janet Halligan graduated from Stowbridge College of Art in 1970. She lived and worked on the south coast until 1984, when she set up a workshop near Nantwich, Cheshire. She makes 'trompe l'oeil' sculptural work - that is everyday objects like bags, shoes, coats, food, handbuilt in stoneware clay and glazed and lustred to look realistic. Recently she has also developed a range of slab-built teapots derived from machine forms. Work is largely handbuilt, mainly in stoneware, and consists chiefly of one-off pieces.

Michael and Barbara Hawkins

Michael and Barbara Hawkins Trained in Cornwall and Bristol. Established present workshop in Gloucestershire in 1979 with Craft Council grant. The pottery is highly decorated stoneware and porcelain, with use of lustres on the more one-off pieces. Range includes bottles, vases, bowls, etc. with subjects such as fish, swans and flowers. The pots are fired in a 90 cu.ft. catenary arch kiln (natural gas) designed and built by Wally Keeler (with help in its construction). Gloss firing to 1280°C, lustre firing to 760°C. Work is sold in galleries throughout the UK with some exported to Germany, Sweden and USA.

Christopher Helson

Christopher Helson born Caracas, Venezuela 1965 one of twins. Studied at Manchester Polytechnic. He is now potting, painting and sculpting.

André Hess

André Hess makes clay objects that refer directly to the history of pottery, yet remain personal and current.

Elaine Hewitt

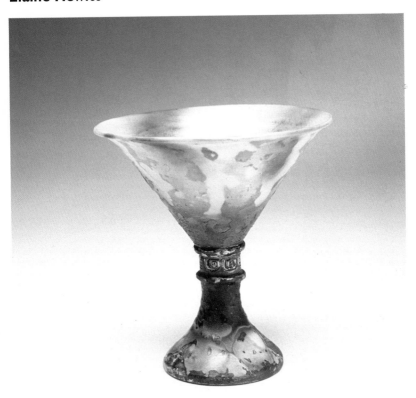

Elaine Hewitt initially studied three dimensional design and ceramics at Guildford School of Art (1967-71). She became a repetition thrower at Grayshott Pottery for six years before setting up her workshop in Frensham in 1992. She completed a BA (Hons) course at West Surrey College of Art and Design and has spent the last two years teaching ceramics part-time at Bedales School, Petersfield. Her work is wheel-thrown using porcelain clay, water-etched using many layers of terra-sigillata and finally saggar fired in a gas kiln. Metals, salts and organic materials added to the sawdust give excitingly unpredictable flashes of colour. Her fascination with ancient, once-buried or entombed vessels is reflected in her work with the resulting decorative effects which suggest age and deterioration.

Andrew Hill

Andrew Hill was born in 1964 in Beaconsfield, Buckinghamshire. After completing his Diploma in Ceramics at Derby Lonsdale in 1985, he began working as a potter in his own studio and workshop in Trawden, Lancashire. The influence of eastern ceramics led him to specialise in thrown work as well as the techniques of raku firing. He works with a variety of materials during the reduction including bracken, ferns and sawdust. The result is a dramatic contrast of vibrant, spontaneous colour against a blackened, carbonised body. His work is widely collected and exhibited throughout the UK and Europe.

Anthony B. Hodge

Anthony B. Hodge B.A. Loughborough College of Art and Design 1969-72. 1981, set up Skyfield Studio. I produce an ever-changing range of one-off bowls, boxes, vases, sculptural forms and murals. Inspired from observation of the countryside and coastline of Britain, emphasis is placed on subtle colours and surface textures. Using a combination of thrown and handbuilding techniques with both T material and porcelain, the clay surfaces are often carved and relief impressed. My own particular glaze recipes have developed over many years and provide some unique reactions and original colour combinations. All fired to Orton cone 10 in a reduced atmosphere mains gas kiln.

Terri Holman

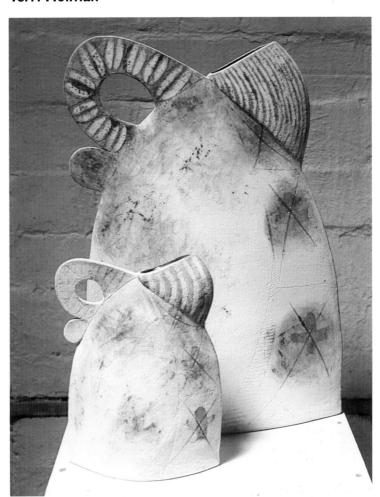

Terri Holman One leaving Cardiff in 1981, after three years at South Glamorgan Institute, I moved to Exeter where a group of artists joined forces to open a deserted railway warehouse as studios. At this time I became a member of Devon Guild of Craftsmen. A move to Torquay enabled me to open my present workshop. The work has developed in two directions over this ten-year period. The smaller porcelain bowls and lidded boxes of intricate enamel decoration contrasts with the larger stoneware bowls and vases where the glazes, enamels and lustres are used more freely.

Paul Jackson

Paul Jackson

Paul Jackson began his training in the early '70s, working part-time with Joanna Constantinidis. He went on to study full-time at Harrow School of Art, qualifying in 1977, followed by a period as pottery supervisor in a South London job creation scheme. During the two years he was there, Paul became senior supervisor of all the craft departments, and began to develop his own ideas for the form and decoration of domestic ware. His work is functional but provides the base for a personal decorative style that goes beyond simple technique.

Eileen Jones

EJ

Eileen Jones began making pots during her training as an art and craft teacher at Goldsmiths' College in the post-war years. She has recently moved to North Devon and has established Chapelgate Pottery in the picturesque village of Chittlehamholt, five miles from South Molton. She makes a range of stoneware domestic pots in very individual glazes and one-off pieces in porcelain.

Jonathan Keep

JK.

Jonathan Keep Born 1958. Studied Natal University, South Africa. Moved to the UK in 1986 and set up a studio in Snape Maltings, Suffolk. Recently moved to nearby Knodishall where I have a studio and showroom. I make a wide range of pots, a standard range of kitchen and tableware, individually decorated domestic ware and large sculptural pots. Working by myself I aim to produce pots that are well crafted, well designed and pleasing to live with.

Judith King

Judith King I started my pottery career as a mature student at the West Surrey College of Art and Design, Farnham in 1985 where I did eighteen months on a B.A. course. I then transferred to Derby College for two years, gaining my H.N.D. in Design Crafts (Studio Ceramics). I work with a white earthenware clay, most of my pottery is handthrown and hand decorated. The designs reflect my own personality: I like freshness, spontaneity, practicalability and decoration. My influences come from my love of flowers (particularly wild flowers), the countryside, gardening, textiles and interior design. I get a lot of pleasure from working as a studio potter and I hope I can pass on some of that pleasure to those who use my pots. I sell my work through shops mainly in Britain and have outlets in Southern Ireland, Channel Isles, Holland and Japan. I work from a small studio at home.

Julian King-Salter

Julian King-Salter Born 1954. Set up as a full-time potter in 1983. Self taught. Makes individual handbuilt stoneware pots using flattenened coils shaped by pinching, without scraping. Own recipe glazes are applied to biscuited ware by brushing, often in layers, and fired to cone 8 or 9 in an electric kiln. Solo exhibitions: Leigh Gallery, London; Royal Exchange, Manchester; Peter Dingley, Stratford; Beaux Arts, Bath; Scottish Gallery, Edinburgh; New Ashgate, Farnham, and Harlequin, Greenwich. Work is regularly supplied to selected galleries around the country.

Gaynor Lindsell

Gaynor Lindsell After several years as head of art in a London comprehensive school, studied and taught ceramics in New York. She set up her own studio on returning to England in 1988 and also worked as an assistant to Colin Pearson. Her work explores flow and movement in the form and seeks to integrate form, surface colour and texture. Her pots are thrown, ribbed and altered. She currently works in low-fired clays and uses the Ancient Greek technique of terra sigillata to produce a subtle surface sheen which is enhanced by burnishing. She enjoys giving workshops and has exhibited in England, France and the USA. Council Member of the Craft Potters Association.

Christine McCole

Christine McCole Trained at Harrow, studio pottery course 1977-79. Together with her partner Roger Brann, set up the pottery in Llanboidy in 1980. Makes raw glazed domestic ware, woodfired to 1280°C in a 40 cu.ft. fast-fire kiln. Member of the Makers Guild in Wales. Pots sold mainly from the workshop.

Vinitha McWhinnie

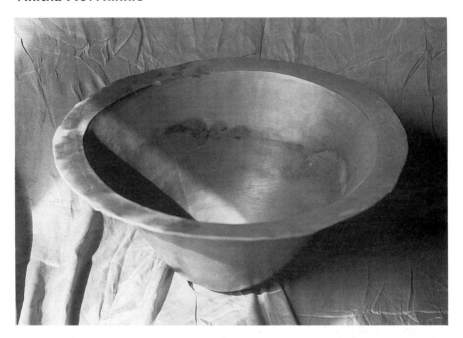

Vinitha McWhinnie Her present ceramics consist of handbuilt, individual vessel forms, burnished after coloured terra sigillata is applied. Decoration is resist-smoking in a garden incinerator using wood shavings. Vinitha read science in Sri Lanka but, although her interest in ceramics started there, training was an apprenticeship in Chelsea. Later having obtained a diploma she travelled extensively observing the pottery in many European countries, India, Japan, Thailand and the USA. The pottery of the Pueblo Indians, ancient Cypriot work, and her own origins influence her current work. She exhibits widely including the C PA, Crafts Council and Bonhams; conducts workshops, teaches, and is setting up an additional studio in the 'Custard Factory' Birmingham, a new arts centre.

Martin McWilliam

Martin McWilliam Born 1957. Bournemouth College of Art 1975-76, Dartington Pottery Workshop 1976-78. Experience in a number of workshops in Europe and Japan 1978-83. In 1983 established own workshop in Germany. 1988, 1989, 1993 Saltglaze Exhibition Koblens, Germany. 1993 Exhibit at the International Craft Fair, München, Cadaquès Spain L'amistat Galeria D'Art, with W. Heinze (painter). 1994 Frankfurst Trienale Museum for Art and Craft, Exhibition goes to Japan 1995. I make saltglaze porcelain domestic ware and coil/slab-built stoneware objects, all wood-fired in a 6 ku/m chamber kiln. "Ever tried/Ever failed/Never mind try again/Fail Better" (S. Beckett).

Made in Cley

MADE IN CLEY

Made in Cley is a crafts cooperative established in 1981 comprising six potters and a jeweller: Wolf Altmann, Gunhild Espelage, Richard Kelham, Rosalind Redfern, Robert Wickens, Barbara Widdup and Quay Proctor-Mears (the jeweller). We produce a very wide range of wheel-thrown, reduction and oxidised-fired stoneware for domestic use and also individual sculptural pieces in stoneware, raku and porcelain. We sell our work in our own gallery which is open throughout the year.

Fenella Mallalieu

Fenella Mallalieu My intention as a potter is to make functional pots for special occasions - pots to give eating a sense of ceremony. I readily admit to a love of throwing and aim to interfere with that as little as possible by keeping turning to a minimum. I am drawn to particular forms - fat bellied jugs, wide bowls, wide rimmed plates and ovals. The latter made by picking up a soft round disc and chucking it across my work table. I mark out my pattern with terracotta slip and then paint and wax those areas before dipping in the background glaze. I work in white earthenware, bisque fired to 1160°C, and have half-a-dozen glazes which are all food safe.

Angela Mellor

Angela Mellor was born in Cheshire. Teacher trained at The Victoria University of Manchester, gaining Distinction in Art and Design. Advanced certificate - Art Education at the University of East Anglia, specialising in ceramics, under Peter Lane. In 1991 set up a studio at home in Cambridge. Her work in bone china has developed as a result of studying under Sasha Wardell in France. Angela exploits the traditional methods of producing bone china resulting in dramatic, translucent, tactile forms inspired by nature. Her work is widely exhibited in this country and also in the USA, France and Germany.

Kate Mellors

Kate Mellors I trained at Camberwell School of Art 1972-75 and on leaving shared a workshop in London and taught part-time in adult education. I made a range of tableware and also individual thrown and decorated pieces. In 1980 I set up a workshop at home and started making stoneware garden pottery in 1985. This new direction arose from my interest in gardens, traditional architecture and garden pottery. Travel in the Far East in 1986 provided further inspiration. The larger scale work needed more space and in 1990 I moved to West Dorset to start a new pottery in a converted farm building. I now work full-time making a range of garden lanterns, bird-baths, planters, stools and fountains. These are all once-fired to 1280°C.

Toff Milway

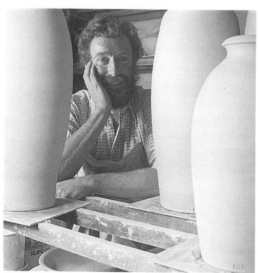

Toff Milway Saltglaze country potter, producing a variety of domestic kitchenware and individual dinner services in saltglaze. Some large decorative pieces. Introduced to saltglaze working with Gwyn Hanssen in France. Extended periods abroad working in Africa and USA. I now live and work in the beautiful Cotswold village of Conderton, and sell all I make from my own studio gallery. Commissions undertaken. Occasional exhibitions. Member of the Gloucestershire Guild of Craftsmen.

Jill Moger

Jill Moger 7/94

Jill Moger   Her love of wildlife, and particular interest in reptiles, has led her to concentrate her ceramics in this field. She endeavours to bring out the very best in her subjects by exaggerating their finer points, thus making each original sculpture unmistakably her own. Intricate details are finely modelled to give a strong sense of realism. Handbuilt sculptures in porcelain or stoneware. Fired to 1260°C in a electric kiln. Various glazes, stains and lustres. Work widely represented in Britain and abroad. Regular exhibitions.

Sarah Monk

SARAH
MONK

Sarah Monk Everything I make has a specific use coupled with a sense of fun and playfulness. For example, I produce a range of breakfast ware including toast-racks, egg cups and cereal bowls designed to start the day on a cheery note. I enjoy the warmth and colour of earthenware glazes and for this reason choose to work in white clay. Graduating from Bath in 1992 I now have a workshop and showroom near Ledbury in Herefordshire.

Roger Mulley

Roger Mulley specialises in large hand-thrown pots which he decorates in a variety of slips and glazes. He especially enjoys throwing 'large ware', many of his pots being 50 or 60 kg in weight. Most of his work is decorated with paper resist and sgraffito designs using coloured slips. Some pots are raw glazed while others are left unglazed to leave a natural matt finish. His range includes both earthenware and stoneware. Roger Mulley makes many individual pieces for private commissions. Work also includes large conservatory glazed planters and decorated garden terracotta. His pots are mainly sold from his workshop at Clanfield Pottery, which he and his wife Sarah established 16 years ago. Roger Mulley's work is now found in many private collectons both in the UK and abroad.

Sue Munday

Sue Munday specialised in ceramics at North Staffordshire Polytechnic in 1986. Since then she has established herself in her own workshop creating reduction fired sculptural vessels. The tactile, stone-like pieces are made from 'T' material and white stoneware which produce a coarse but plastic body. The method of of hand-building, the use of slips, and latex with the colour coming from the inside glazing are all combined to enhance the form.

Stephen Murfitt

SM
STEPHEN MURFITT
CERAMICS

Stephen Murfitt Educated at Cambridge School of Art, Farnham College of Art and the Middlesex Polytechnic (Hornsey College) from 1972-78. Currently setting up new workshop in Cambridgeshire having been based in Wiltshire for the last ten years. The pots are handbuilt and raku-fired and have been exhibited and included in many private and public collections.

Tessa Wolfe Murray

TWM

T. Wolfe Murray

Tessa Wolfe Murray trained at Goldsmiths' College 1982-84. Vases and dishes are slab-built, and candlesticks slip-cast in red earthenware. They are decorated with slips, stains and glazes and fired twice in an electric kiln. The final low temperature smoking is achieved in an open sawdust kiln. Flat shapes with a soft elliptical curve, like cardboard cut-outs when seen from a distance, are contradicted by the illusory depths of the surface decoration which suggest desert landscapes or cloud-strewn skies. Exhibits and sells to galleries in the UK, Germany and Holland.

Christine Niblett

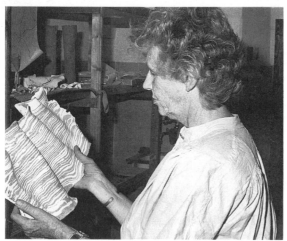

Christine Niblett Born in Cheshire but moved to live in Palma de Mallorca in 1966. Initial studies included four years at the Palma School of Applied Arts (Ceramics). Now working solely in laminated millefiore porcelain, body-stained with natural metal oxides and reduction-fired to 1260°C. The Mediterranean environment has a great influence in the flowing patterns and clear colours integrated into delicate forms. Enjoys participating in exhibitions, symposia and competitions in Europe, which have included Arte-Fiera, Bologna; Ob'Art, Paris; Siklos International Ceramics Symposium and Kecskemet International Ceramic Studio, both Hungary; International Biennial of Ceramic Art, Vallauris (1988,1990, 1992, 1994).

Jacqueline Norris

Jacqueline Norris trained on the Harrow Pottery Course and the Royal College of Art. I recently moved to Eton High Street near Windsor Bridge and my work sells through Eton Applied Arts, our small contemporary crafts gallery linked to the studio, as well as the Craft Council Shop and other galleries. I work with T-material usually mixed with porcelain. This gives a whiteness which reflects the intense colours of my matt and satin glazes. I use an oxidation firing to cone 8.

Carol Peevor

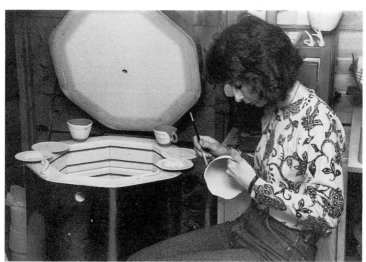

Carol Peevor

Carol Peevor I was born in 1953 at Ironbridge in Shropshire. I studied ceramics at Wolverhampton Polytechnic 1976-79. I now live and work in Wednesbury in the West Midlands. My working space is small and luckily so are my pots. I make a range of one-off forms which are built in press moulds. There seems to be no limit to the ideas I have for pattern and additions to the forms. My range includes lidded jars, dishes, spoons and bowls. I use white stoneware clay and decorate with oxides and underglaze colours.

Nancy Pickard

Nancy Pickard Born in 1963 in Sao Paulo, Brazil. I spent my childhood in the Channel Islands before attending what was then the Central School of Art, and the Cardiff Institute. Now working from my studio in Cardiff, I produce individually designed pieces available at many outlets throughout the UK. I enjoy handling plastic clay with the minimum of complicated equipment but always trying to preserve a fresh, unworked form and surface. Parts of the pots are made by rolling flat slabs, texturing them and then bending them to form handles, spouts etc.   The inspiration of the work is the organic: the natural geometry of plants and animals and the evolution of functional form. This is probably why there is such an animated quality to the pots. Whilst all the pieces are intended to be displayed in a domestic environment, some are closer to the traditionally functional than others. A list of outlets and information pack is available on request.

Philomena Pretsell

P.M.P.

Philomena Pretsell Edinburgh College of Art 1987-89 (BA Hons) Diploma in Post-Graduate Studies 1989-1990. All Pretsell's work is slab built, slip decorated earthenware. Building pots with slabs gives tremendous scope to the imagination and the variations are endless. By decorating on the slab first, the clay can be treated like a piece of fabric and the pattern and form fall naturally into place when assembled. Transfers are becoming increasingly important. They have a humble beauty which is invariably disregarded as they are applied to unimaginative cool surfaces. The skills of their creators dismissed and rejected by many. Of the transfers Pretsell enthuses 'I love using them, they have a wonderful quality of decorativeness and a hint of nostalgia.'

Gaynor Reeve

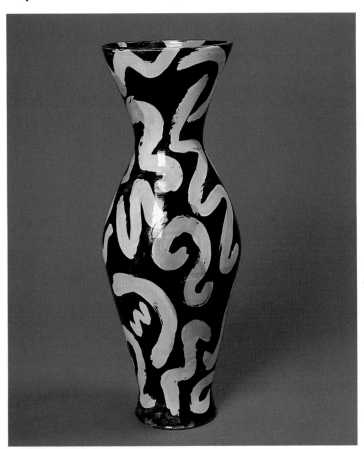

Gaynor Reeve I have explored most aspects of ceramics since I began in 1982, but my love of colour has influenced my present style. I use white earthenware to produce wall plates and large vases, both of which are thrown. Having an interest in asbstract art my designs are usually bold, bright and colourful. I use many coloured slips and freely decorate with various sized brushes and sponges. In an electric kiln, I biscuit fire to 1130°C and then fire to 1080°C with a clear glaze. I gain immense pleasure and satisfaction in creating individual pieces.

Audrey Richardson

Audrey Richardson trained originally in painting and sculpture at Duncan of Jordanstone College of Art, Dundee, Scotland. Started potting through attending local evening classes. Works alone, making individual pots and sculptures. These are handbuilt using mainly T-material, then decorated with a selected range of slips and glazes. The work is fired to 1250°C. Also undertakes large garden sculptures and portraits on commission. Has recently moved house and workshop to scenic Pembrokeshire. Showcase of current work on display.

Michael and Wendy Salt

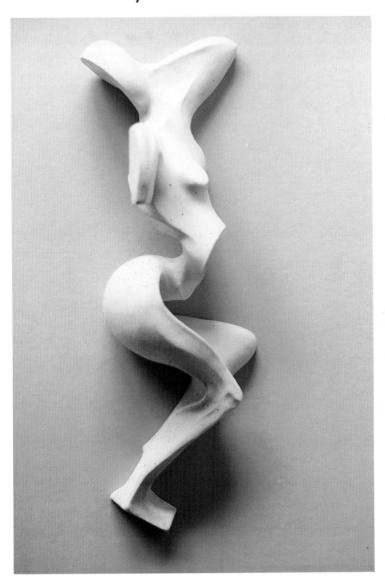

Michael and Wendy Salt Present studio workshop and showroom opened in 1979, We work individually on ceramic sculpture, paintings and drawings and together on hand-thrown stoneware vessels.

Nicolette Savage

Nicolette Savage N.D.D; A.T.C. from Goldsmiths' in ceramics and printmaking. I make mainly large, handbuilt urns and planters for conservatory and garden, featuring strong drawing and design. I use craft crank washed with oxides to give contrast to the carved and incised decoration, then fired to 1260°C. Natural forms and repeating motifs are an abiding fascination. I am currently absorbed in water features, which are self-contained, often with planting spaces. The elements of moving water, clay and plants combined give me great creative stimulus. Part-time teacher of pottery and printmaking in Adult Education (Bromley).

Sheila Seepersaud-Jones

Sheila Seepersaud-Jones Born in Guyana. I taught English before coming to England to train as a nurse. Later I developed my interest in art and achieved a BA Hons in Fine Art, St.Martins School of Art, London. As initially I was concerned with exploration of three dimensional forms I chose to do my degree in sculpture. Latterly I have concentrated on clay to explore texture, colour and pattern on three dimensional surfaces. Work is both sculptural and traditional. I make coiled, slabbed and thrown pots fired at 1100°C - 1250°C. I hand paint my pieces in designs which reflect my Caribbean and European backgrounds.

Graham Skinner

GS

Graham Skinner I studied at Medway College of Art and Design during 1984-88. Set up my present studio in Rochester in 1989. Most of my work is thrown and vessel orientated. At present the exteriors of my pots are glazed with a dry matt finish using a variety of glazes and slips stained with different oxides. I have a keen interest in glaze experimentation and I am always testing for new glazes. My work is fired in a propane kiln in oxidised and reduced atmospheres to cone 9. I am also a part-time ceramic technician at the Kent Institute of Art and Design.

Charles Spacey

Charles Spacey Born in North Wales. Studied ceramics at Farnham (W.S.C.A.D. 1972-75). Worked as assistant in various workshops both in UK and Continent. In 1979 started own workshop in Switzerland with Brigitte Spacey. Moved workshop to Mid-Wales near Welshpool in 1993. At the moment working mainly on slab built stoneware. Teapots, plates and vases decorated by glazing geometrically and visually illusory inspired patterns fired to 1300°C in a reducing atmosphere. Has exhibited widely on Continent including the exhibitions at Faenza and Vallauris.

Peter Sparrey

Peter Sparrey Specialising in thrown raku ceramics.

Chris Speyer

YERJA

Chris Speyer   Trained as a theatre designer and worked in theatre for many years. Now, as the ceramic half of Yerja Ceramics & Textiles, makes thrown and press moulded stoneware. Work exhibited and sold throughout the UK and abroad.

Christel Spriet

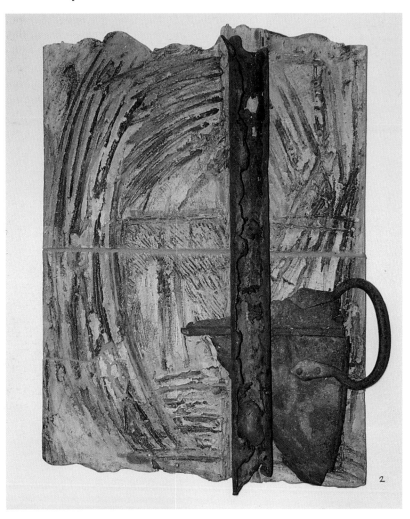

2

Christel Spriet studied ceramics at Sint-Lucas Institute for Fine Art in Gent, Belgium. She moved to England in 1986 after graduation. She makes stoneware vessels and wall sculptures combining drift-wood, corroded metal and ceramics. Different layers of oxide underglaze enamels, slips and glazes are used to achieve the final result.

Rebecca Taylor

Rebecca Taylor Her pots are generally unglazed, heavily textured and oxidised in either earthy and mossy colours or metallic and spangled hues, thus giving respectively an ancient or medieval appearance. Using unusual methods she obtains unorthodox finishes sometimes firing straight to stone to retain colour and 'feel'. Her latticed pieces bring a new dimension to potting with an almost metallic ring to them. Her experiments with life forms and strange textures have created a new look which is both functional and sculptural which have made her popular in both Spain and Greece.

Lyndon Thomas

Lyndon Thomas Born 1941. I have received no formal training in pottery, the skills being accumulated by means of voracious reading and endless practice. In 1967 I set up my first workshop and supply work to various craft outlets. All work is thrown with functional shapes predominating; I obtain greatest satisfaction from making jugs, storage jars and shallow bowls. The bulk of production is oxidised stoneware fired to a maximum temperature of 1270°C in a 12 cu.ft. electric kiln. The clay is grogged stoneware produced by Spencroft, suitable for large and small scale work. Glazes are developed from various recipes with iron being the main colourant.

Katrina Trinick

Katrina Trinick Born in Cornwall 1950. Dip.A.D. Ceramics at Central School of Art and Design 1969-72. My present workshop was set up in 1991. All work is handbuilt - coiled, pinched and press-moulded, in a white body which, after firing in an electric kiln, is smoked, producing random colours from black through browns to pale greys and buff. The smoking and the feel of the burnished surface suits the organic forms which are inspired by shells, pebbles and fossils. The scale of work ranges from small pots and jewellery to large coiled vessels.

Tydd Pottery

Tydd Pottery We make a range of hand-thrown, oil-fired, terracotta garden pots.

Sue Varley

SV

Sue Varley

Sue Varley I studied at the Bath Academy of Art, where I specialised in ceramics and was taught by James Tower. I make both earthenware and stoneware pots. Some of my ideas for form and decoration coming from looking at landscape, rock formations, strata, etc. The colours found in stones and pebbles are often a starting point for clays and glazes - I mix oxides and/or grog into the basic clay body. The earthenware pots are first fired in an electric kiln and then smoked in sawdust, newspaper and grasses, I use mixed wood ash glazes for my stoneware pots and fire 1250°C in an electric kiln.

Carol Wainwright

Carol Wainwright trained as a painter at Harrow School of Art in the late '50s and two decades later in ceramics at West Surrey College of Art and Design. Whilst still a student she established her workshop and built a gas kiln. Clay she buys 'as dug'. Much of her making has been bowls and plates, which have provided suitable surfaces for vigorously brushed decoration, built from multiple layers of coloured. A recent move to Dorset has necessitated rebuilding the kiln which is now larger, providing the opportunity to further develop larger forms.

Andrew Watts

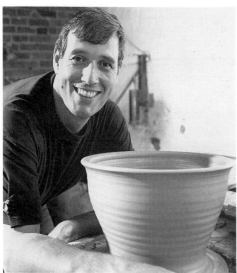

Andrew Watts trained at Camberwell School of Art. After working in Battersea, he moved his pottery to north Hertfordshire in 1981 and became Lannock Pottery. This has grown slowly, moving into the present premises in Weston, near Hitchin in 1992. Here he works with three others making thrown and cast 'Stonewares for houses and gardens'. The range spreads from garden planters and water features to vases and table lamps and oven-to-tableware. He also makes some one-off pieces.

Nicola Werner

NW· 94·

Nicola Werner All the pots are thrown in red Fremington earthenware clay, biscuit fired and dipped in tin glaze, then painted in oxides with colourful hens, birds, leaves and flowers. I love majolica for everyday pots and tiles and produce quite a wide range which is available direct from the workshop or at selected galleries including the Victoria and Albert Museum Shop.

David Constantine White

or signed David

David Constantine White began the pottery in 1981 to use local earthenware clay. Making a constantly changing range of decorative domestic earthenware, using majolica technique on semi-transparent glaze, similar to Batik. In 1993 invited to ceramics workshop in Tokoname, Japan.

George Wilson

George Wilson

GW

George Wilson took early retirement from full-time teaching at the Richmond Adult College (where he was the founder of the Ceramics Department) in order to devote more time to producing his own work in his Ealing, West London studio. He continues to teach part-time at Brunel University and Surbiton College. He works mainly in reduction and oxidised stoneware and in lustred porcelain, producing individual decorative pieces for interior designers and architects, and containers for Ikebana flower arranging. George exhibits widely in the UK and sells work in America and Europe. He aims to have at least one major solus exhibition a year. He is currently designing and producing a range of pottery exclusive to leading London stores.

Karen Ann Wood

Karen Ann Wood makes a range of table and ovenware - some oxidised, some reduced - in a gas fired kiln. Currently has an especial interest in shino-type glazes. Trained in Canada, New Zealand and the UK after gaining a B.A. from the University of Western Australia. Teaches ceramics part-time and has worked from the same studio since 1978.

Gill Wright

Gill Wainwright works in red earthenware and makes handbuilt pots which are burnished and sawdust fired.

Addresses of Fellows

Adrian Abberley
95a Sheen Road
Richmond-upon-Thames
Surrey

(0181) 948 1234

Please telephone

Tim Andrews
Woodbury Pottery
Greenway
Woodbury
Exeter
Devon EX5 1LW

(01395) 233475

Showroom usually open Mon-Sat 10am-6pm, but it is advisable to telephone if making special journey

Mick Arnup
Holtby Pottery
Holtby
York YO1 3UA

(01904) 489377

Showroom open 10.00-18.00 every day. Holtby is five miles from York on A166

Keith Ashley
Farleigh Studios
Farleigh Place
Farleigh Road
London N16 7SX

(0171) 267 9032

Visitors welcome but please telephone first

Chris Aston
Chris Aston Pottery
4 High Street
Elkesley
nr. Retford
Nottinghamshire DN22 8AJ

Tel/Fax (01777) 838 391

The village of Elkesley, once part of the estates belonging to the Dukes of Newcastle on the edge of Sherwood Forest, is on the A1, 20 miles north of Newark and only 20 minutes drive from Ruffford.

Visitors are always welcome to the workshop and gallery showroom, generally open 7 days a week, 10am to 6pm

Felicity Aylieff
37 Kensington Gardens
Bath BA1 6LH

Tel. (01225) 334136 Fax. (01225) 313492

Visitors welcome but by appointment only

Svend Bayer
Duckpool Cottage
Sheepwash
Beaworthy
Devon EX21 5PW

(0140 923) 282

Pottery always open. Visitors welcome but best to telephone first

Michael Bayley
Beechcroft Cottage
Green Lane
Temple Ewell
Dover
Kent CT16 3AS

(01304) 822624

Visitors are welcome. Please telephone for directions

Peter Beard
The Pottery
Bottom Pond Road
Wormshill
nr Sittingbourne
Kent ME9 0TR

(01622 884) 554

Studio open at any reasonable time. Visitors very welcome but must make an appointment

Beverley Bell-Hughes
Fron Dirion
Conwy Road
Llandudno Junction
Gwynedd LL31 9AY

(01492) 572575

Visitors by appointment only

Terry Bell-Hughes
Fron Dirion
Conwy Road
Llandudno Junction
Gwynedd LL31 9AY

(01492) 572575

Visitors by appointment only

Maggie Angus Berkowitz
21-23 Park Road
Milnthorpe
Cumbria LA7 7AD
(015395) 63970
Welcomes visitors by appointment

Sebastian Blackie
Thornfield
Bentley
nr Farnham
Surrey GU10 5NF
(01420) 22209
Visitors welcome by appointment only

Clive Bowen
Shebbear Pottery
Shebbear
Beaworthy
Devon EX21 5QZ
(01409) 281271
Wholesale and retail customers are welcome at the showroom

Loretta Braganza
The Coach House
198 Mount Vale
York YO2 2DL
(01904) 630454
Visitors by appointment only

Carlo Briscoe & Edward Dunn
Gwaith Menyn
Llanglydwen
Whitland
Dyfed SA34 0XP
Tel/Fax (01994) 419402
Visitors welcome but please telephone first

Sandy Brown
Anchorage
3 Marine Parade
Appledore
Bideford
Devon EX39 1PJ
(01237) 478219
Usually open: please telephone first to make sure

Deirdre Burnett
48 Gipsy Hill
London SE19 1NL

Ian Byers
10 Westbourne Road
Croydon
CR0 6HP
(0181) 654 0225
Visitors are welcome by appointment

Alan Caiger-Smith
The Pottery
Aldermaston
Berkshire RG7 4LW
(01734) 713359
Open only by appointment

John Calver
23 Silverdale Road
Yealand Redmayne
Carnforth
Lancs. LA5 9TA
(01524) 781362
Visitors are welcome to the workshop but please telephone first

Seth Cardew
Wenford Bridge Pottery
St. Breward
Bodmin
Cornwall PL30 3PN
(01208) 850471
Visitors welcome by appointment

Daphne Carnegy
Kingsgate Workshops
110-116 Kingsgate Road
London NW6
(0171) 328 2051
Visitors welcome by appointment

Michael Casson
Wobage Farm
Upton Bishop
Ross-on-Wye
Herefordshire HR9 7QP
(01989) 780 233
Showroom open 10am-5pm on Saturdays and Sundays. Other times please telephone first

Sheila Casson
Wobage Farm
Upton Bishop
Ross-on-Wye
Herefordshire HR9 7QP

(01989) 780 233

Showroom open 10am-5pm on Saturdays and
Sundays. Other times please telephone first

Linda Chew
42 Cheriton Road
Winchester
Hampshire SO22 5AY

(01962) 867218

Visitors welcome but please telephone first

Jenny Clarke
25 Etloe Road
Westbury Park
Bristol BS6 7NZ

(0117) 9735193

Visitors welcome by appointment

Derek Clarkson
1 The Poplars
Bacup
Lancashire OL13 8AD

(01706) 874541

Visitors welcome, telephone first if possible

Margery Clinton
The Pottery
Newton Port
Haddington
East Lothian

(0162) 082 3584

Pottery and showroom usually open part of each day
except Sunday and Monday, but visitors are advised to
telephone to confirm

Peter Clough
34 Dragon View
Harrogate
N. Yorkshire HG1 4DG

(01423) 506700 (Home)
(01904) 616714 (Work)

Visitors by prior arrangement only

Russell Coates
10 The Butts
Frome
Somerset BA11 4AA

(01373) 452443

Visitors welcome but please telephone first

Roger Cockram
Chittlehampton Pottery
Victoria House
Chittlehampton
North Devon EX37 9PX

(01769) 540420

Vistors welcome 9am-6pm weekdays. Usually also
weekends, but best telephone first

Barbara Colls
177 Thunder Lane
Thorpe St Andrew
Norwich NR7 0JF

(01603) 36695

No showroom but visitors welcome by appointment

Joanna Constantinidis
2 Bells Chase
Great Baddow
Chelmsford
Essex CM2 8DT

(01245) 471842

Visitors by appointment

Delan Cookson
Lissadell
St Buryan
Penzance
Cornwall TR19 6HP

(01736) 810347

Visitors welcome at showroom/workshop by
appointment

Bennett Cooper
Mistley Quay Workshops
Mistley
Manningtree
Essex CO11 1HB

(01206) 393884

Showroom open seven days a week
10am - 6pm

Emmanuel Cooper
Fonthill Pottery
38 Chalcot Road
London NW1 8LP
(0171) 722 9090
Visitors welcome by appointment

Gilles Le Corre
19 Howard Street
Oxford OX4 3AY
(01865) 245 289
Visitors by appointment

Dartington Pottery
Shinners Bridge
Dartington
Totnes
Devon TQ9 6JE
(01803) 864163
Shop opening hours Monday-Saturday
10.00am - 6.00pm

Clive Davies
Valley Barn
Homersfield
Harleston
Norfolk IP20 0NS
(01986) 788144
Visitors welcome to studio but please telephone first
to avoid disappointment

Derek Davis
Duff House
Maltravers Street
Arundel
West Sussex BN18 9AP
(01903) 882600
Visitors by appointment

Peter and Jill Dick
Coxwold Pottery
Coxwold
York YO6 4AA
(0134 76) 344
Visitors are welcome to visit the pottery showroom
and see work in progress.
Opening times: Tuesday till Friday and Summer
Sundays 2.00-5.00pm. As there are normally only the
two of us it is wise to telephone before making a
special journey. Group visits by appointment only.

Mike Dodd
'Wellrash'
Boltongate
nr Wigton
Cumbria CA5 1DH
(016973) 71615
Showroom open most of the time, but advisable to
ring first

Jack Doherty
Hooks Cottage
Lea Bailey
Ross-on-Wye
Herefordshire HR9 5TY
(01989) 750644
Visitors are welcome at the workshop and showroom,
please telephone first

John Dunn
Open Studios
168 Kings Road Arches
Brighton,
Sussex BN1 1NB
Tel. (01273) 725013 Fax. (01273) 732626
Visitors welcome by appointment

Geoffrey Eastop
The Potteery
Ecchinswell
nr Newbury
Berkshire RG15 8TT
(01635) 298220
Open most days by appointment

Derek Emms
Mossfield Cottage
Hayes Bank
Stone
Staffs. ST15 8SZ
(01785) 812048
Visitors welcome by appointment only

Dorothy Feibleman
10 Arlingford Road
London SW2 2SU
(0181) 674 8979
Visitors welcome by appointment

Ray Finch
Winchcombe Pottery
Broadway Road
Winchcombe
Cheltenham
Glos. GL54 5NU

(01242) 602462

Open all year Monday-Friday 9.00am-5.00pm
Saturday 10.00am-4.00pm (Showroom only)
May-September Sunday Noon-4.00pm
(Showroom only)

Jutka Fischer
84 Chapel Street
Newhaven
East Sussex BN9 9QD

(01273) 516131

Visitors welcome by appointment only

Robert Fournier
Ashley Groom
Ashley House
Box
Wiltshire SN14 9AN

(01225) 742416

Fournier Pottery. Robert Fournier entered the Central
School of Arts and Crafts 1945/6 under Dora
Billington and became technical and teaching assistant
in 1947. Built and set up Ducketts Wood Pottery,
Hertfordshire, 1946/47 making slipware, tin-glaze and,
later, mosaics. Started the Pottery Department at
Goldsmiths' College 1948, stonewares, with Sheila, at
Potteries in Greenwich, Castle Hill in Kent, and for
fourteen years at Lacock, Wiltshire. Part-time
teaching until 1968 at Chaucer and Maidstone College
of Art. Council Member of the Craft Potters
Association for several years organising three film
festivals. Made several films with John Anderson
including 'Isaac Button', 'Creatures in Clay' (Rosemary
Wren), 'Raku, English style', 'David Leach' etc. and
issued five-hundred slides on pottery. Books include
three in dictionary form *Practical Pottery* (3rd Edition
1992), *Pottery Form* and *Pottery Decoration*, also
Electric Kiln Construction, etc. Initiated and ran Craft
Potters Association Archives 1975-87. **Sheila Fournier**
trained at Goldsmiths' College. London and has potted
professionally since 1961 making stonewares, inlaid and
other porcelain and some sawdust fired and raku
ware. Made several hundred drawings for the books.

Sylvia Des Fours
Heather Hill
Givons Grove
Leatherhead
Surrey KT22 8LB

(01372) 372473

Visitors welcome by appointment

David Frith
Brookhouse Pottery & Malt House Gallery
Brookhouse Lane
Denbigh
Clwyd LL16 4RE

(01745) 812805

Showroom open 10am-6pm six days.
Telephone for Sundays, mostly open in season

Margaret Frith
Brookhouse Pottery & Malt House Gallery
Brookhouse Lane
Denbigh
Clwyd LL16 4RE

(01745) 812805

Showroom open 10am-6pm six days.
Telephone for Sundays, mostly open in season

Tessa Fuchs
24 Cross Road
Kingston-upon-Thames
Surrey KT2 6HG

(0181) 549 6906

Visitors by appointment only

Tony Gant
53 Southdean Gardens
Southfield
London SW19 6NT

(0181) 789 4518

Small showroom - Monday to Saturday 10am-5pm.
Please telephone before calling. Trade enquiries
welcome.

Carolyn Genders
Heatherwood West
Sandy Lane
Crawley Down
Sussex RH10 4HR

(01342) 712987

Visitors welcome to workshop by prior arrangement

John Gibson
Gibson Keremik
Kildevad 6
3760 Gudhjem
Bornholm
Denmark

Tel: Denmark 56498231

We run courses throughout the year dealing with
saltglaze and decoration techniques. Write or
telephone for details.

Christopher Green
34 Northover Road
Westbury-on-Trym
Bristol   BS9 3LL
(0117) 9500852)
Visitors by appointment

Ian Gregory
The Studio
Crumble Cottage
Ansty
Dorchester
Dorset DT2 7PN
(01258) 880891
Workshop and studio open 2.00-6.00pm weekdays.
9.00am-6.00pm Weekends, or by arrangement

Frank Hamer
Llwyn-On
Croes-yn-y-Pant
Mamhilad
Pontypool
Gwent NP4 8RE
(01495) 785700
Visitors welcome preferably by appointment

Jane Hamlyn
Millfield Pottery
Everton
nr Doncaster
S. Yorks DN10 5DD
(01777) 817 723
Visitors welcome - telephone first if possible

Alan Heaps
Minhafren
Aberbechan
Newtown
Powys SY16 3AW
(01686) 630644
Workshop is open at any reasonable time

Joan Hepworth
Westcott Pottery
Robin Cottage
Stones Lane
Westcott
nr Dorking
Surrey RH4 3QH
(01306) 880392
Visitors welcome by appointment. Does not employ
assistants or trainees.

Karin Hessenberg
72 Broomgrove Road
Sheffield S10 2NA
(0114) 2661610
128 Robey Street
Sheffield S4 8JG (studio)

John Higgins
32 Seaman Close
Park Street
St. Albans
Herts. AL2 2NX
(01727) 874299
Visitors welcome by appointment

Ashley Howard
33 Sandling Lane
Penenden Heath
Maidstone
Kent ME14 2HS
(01622) 673807
Visitors by appointment

Joanna Howells
30 School Street
Church Lawford
Rugby CV23 9EE
(01203) 544346
Visitors welcome by appointment

Anita Hoy
50 Julian Avenue
Acton
London W3 9JF
(0181) 992 4041
Visitors by appointment only

John Huggins
Courtyard Pottery
Groundwell Farm
Cricklade Road
Swindon
Wiltshire SN2 5AU
(01793) 7277466
Workshop showroom open Monday - Saturday
9.00am-5.30pm. Summer Sundays 1-5pm

Anne James
Ashleigh
Gloucester Street
Painswick
Gloucestershire GL6 6QN
(01452) 81 3378
Visitors welcome, please telephone first

John Jelfs
The Pottery
Clapton Row
Bourton-on-the-Water
Gloucestershire GL34 2DN

(01451) 820173

Showroom open 9.00am-6.00pm Monday to Saturday

Ruth King
Rose Cottage
Main Street
Shipton-by-Beningbrough
York YO6 1AB

(01904) 470196

Visitors welcome by appointment

Chris Jenkins
19 Towngate
Marsden
Huddersfield
Yorkshire HD7 6DD

(01484) 844444
La Haute Neziérè
St. Julien de Terroux
53110 Lassay
France

(00 33) 43085950

Visitors welcome by appointment

Gabriele Koch
147 Archway Road
London N6 5BL

(0181) 292 3169

Visitors welcome by appointment

Anna Lambert
Chapel Road
Steeton
W. Yorks BD20 6NU

(01535) 657003

Visitors welcome but please write or telephone first

Wendy Johnson
92 Nottingham Road
New Basford
Notts NG7 7AH

(0115) 9607940

Visitors welcome by appointment

Nigel Lambert
Golden Valley Cottage
Morse Lane
Drybrook
Gloucestershire
GL17 9BA

(01594) 542251

No showroom, but visitors welcome; please telephone first

Hazel Johnston
The Croft
North Street
Marton
Rugby
Warwickshire CV23 9RJ

(01926) 632467

Visitors welcome by appointment

Peter Lane
Ivy House
New Alresford
Hampshire SO24 9JU

(01962) 735041

Visitors welcome by appointment

David Jones
18 Willes Terrace
Leamington Spa
Warwicks. CV31 1DL

Tel/Fax: (01926) 314643
Visitors are welcome by appointment only

Richard Launder
35 St Georges Road
Farnham
Surrey GU9 8NA

(01252) 725794

Visitors welcome by appointment only

Walter Keeler
Moorcroft Cottage
Penallt
Monmouth
Gwent NP5 4AH

(01600) 713 946

Visitors welcome but please telephone first

David Leach OBE
Lowerdown Pottery
Bovey Tracey
Devon TQ13 9LE

(01626) 833408

Visitors are welcome at showroom
9.00am-6.00pm weekdays,
Saturdays 9.00am-1.00pm by appointment only

Janet Leach
Leach Pottery
St Ives
Cornwall TR26 2HE
(01736) 796398

Showroom open 10.00am-5.00pm weekdays
Summer season and holidays 10.00am-5.00pm.
Other times by request

John Leach
Muchelney Pottery
nr Langport
Somerset TA10 0DW
(01458) 250324

Shop open (all year round)
Monday-Friday 9.00am-1.00pm, 2.00-5.00pm;
Saturday 9.00am-1.00pm. Workshop viewing by prior
telephone appointment please. Kiln firing may be
viewed on advertised Open Days.

Eileen Lewenstein
11 Western Esplanade
Portslade
Brighton
East Sussex BN41 1WE
(01273) 418705

Visitors welcome by appointment

Martin Lewis
110c Lynncroft
Eastwood
Notts. NG16 3ES
(01773) 710501

No showroom; visitors welcome but please telephone
first

Laurence McGowan
6 Aughton
Collingbourne Kingston
Marlborough
Wilts SN8 3SA
(01264) 850 749

Visitors by appointment please

Mal Magson
45 North Leas Avenue
Scarborough
YO12 6LJ
(01723) 362969

Visitors by appointment only

Jim Malone
Hagget House
Towngate
Ainstable
Carlisle
Cumbria CA4 9RE
(01768) 896444

Showroom open daily from 9am onwards. Visitors to
workshop by appointment

John Maltby
The Orchard House
Stoneshill
Crediton
Devon EX17 4EF
(01363) 772753

Visitors welcome at any reasonable time. Please
telephone first

West Marshall
118 White Hill
Chesham
Buckinghamshire
HP5 1AR
(01494) 785969

Very small workshop - visitors welcome by
appointment only please

Will Levi Marshall
Orchardton Pottery
Auchencairn
Castle Douglas
Dumfries & Galloway
DG7 1QL, Scotland
(01556) 640399

Visitors by appointment only

Leo Francis Matthews
Ivy Court
Shawbury
nr Shrewsbury
Shropshire SY4
(01903) 250 866

Visitors by appointment only

Marcio Mattos
40 Sydner Road
Stoke Newington
London N16 7UG
Tel/Fax (0171) 254 1351

Visitors welcome by appointment

Peter Meanley
6 Downshire Road
Bangor
Co. Down
N. Ireland
BT20 3TW

(01247) 466831

Visitors welcome, but please telephone first

Eric James Mellon
5 Parkfield Avenue
Bognor Regis
West Sussex PO21 3BW

(01243) 263221

Clients by appointment

Jon Middlemiss
Wheal Vor Cottage
Tyringham Road
Leland, St Ives
Cornwall TR26 3LF

(01736) 754832

Visitors by appointment only

David Miller
Rue du Ranc
30190 Collorgues
France

(00 33) 66 81 91 19
and
33 St Andrew's Square
Surbiton
Surrey KT6 4EG

Visitors welcome; write or telephone beforehand

Ursula Mommens
The Pottery
South Heighton
Newhaven
Sussex BN9 0HL

(01273) 514408 or 514330

Open every day 9am-6pm

Aki Moriuchi
1 Parkside Drive
Edgware
Middlesex HA8 8JU

(0181) 958 2639

Visitors by appointment

Emily Myers
3rd Floor
3/11 Westland Place
London N1 7LP

(0171) 250 3008

Visitors by appointment only Correspondence to:
68 Kensington Park Road
London W11 3BJ

Susan Nemeth
Westland Studios
3rd Floor
Westland Place
London N1 7LP

(0171) 250 3224/249 0102

Visitors by appointment only

Lawson Oyekan
7 Cotswold Gardens
East Ham
London E6 6HZ

(0181) 472 6976

Colin Pearson
3 Mountfort Terrace
Barnsbury Square
London N1 1JJ

(0171) 607 1965
Workshop & gallery
15-17 Cloudesley Road
London N1 0EL

The studio and gallery are a short walk from the
Angel, Islington, or the Crafts Council Gallery,
Pentonville Road. Transport by Underground: Angel.
By bus: 73, 19, 38, 171 or 4. Cars should approach via
Copenhagen Street. Visitors to the gallery are
welcome, but should confirm between 8 and 9am the
day of intended visit, or between 6 and 10pm the
night before.

Jane Perryman
102 Sturton Street
Cambridge CB1 2QF

(01223) 312301

Visitors are welcome by appointment only

Richard Phethean
76 Oglander Road
London SE15 4EN

(0171) 639 1521

Visitors welcome by arrangement

Anthony Phillips
23a Iliffe Yard
Crampton Street
London SE17 3QA

(0171) 703 1490

Visitors welcome by appointment

Peter Phillips
Ivy Cottage
Taylors Lane
Trottiscliffe
Kent ME19 5DS

(01732) 822901

La Reynie
Murcurol
Commune de Borreze
Salignac 24590
Dordogne, France

(00 33) 53 28 93 31

Visitors welcome, by appointment, at either studio

Ian Pirie
8 St Michael's Place
Newton Hill
Stonehaven
Kincardineshire

(01569) 730908

John Pollex
White Lane Gallery
1 White Lane
Barbican
Plymouth
Devon PL1 2LP

(01752) 662338

Gallery open throughout the year 10.00am-5.00pm.
Visitors to the workshop by appointment

Vicki Read
'Church Green'
Bickleigh
Tiverton
Devon EX16 8RH

(01884) 855 657

Stanislas Reychan MBE
757 The White House
Albany Street
London NW1 3UP

(0171) 387 1200 Ext. 757

Born in 1897 in Vienna of Polish parents. Granted
MBE for war service. After the war studied Modelling
and Pottery at St. Martin's School of Art and the
Central School of Arts and Crafts in London. From
1953 worked in his studio in St. Johns Wood. He

exhibited in the Royal Academy, Paris Salon and the
Polish National Museum in Wroclaw. When retiring
he was granted Honorary Membership of the CPA.

As an author he published in Kracaw *A Diary of a
Strange Man: From Lwow to London* and in London in
1993 *Playing with Dolls*

Mary Rich
Penwerris Pottery
Cowlands Creek
Old Kea
nr Truro
Cornwall TR3 6AT

(01872) 76926

There is no showroom, but visitors are welcome by
prior appointment

Christine-Ann Richards
Chapel House
High Street
Wanstrow
Shepton Mallet
Somerset BA4 4TB

(01749) 850 208

Visitors to the workshop by appointment only

David Roberts
Cressfield House
44 Upperthong Lane
Holmfirth
Huddersfield
West Yorkshire HD7 1BQ

(01484) 685110

No showroom but visitors are welcome to workshop
by appointment

Jim Robison
Booth House Gallery
3 Booth House
Holmfirth
Huddersfield
W. Yorkshire HD7 1QA

(01484) 685270

Studio and Gallery open to the public at weekends
and by appointment

Phil Rogers
Marston Pottery
Lower Cefn Faes
Rhayader
Powys LD6 5LT

(01597) 810875

Workshop and showroom half-mile from village
centre. Signposted from car park. Visitors welcome
at workshop at any reasonable time

Duncan Ross
Daneshay House
71 Alma Lane
Hale
Farnham
Surrey GU9 0LT
(01252) 710704
Visitors to showroom welcome; please telephone

Antonia Salmon
20 Adelaide Road
Nether Edge
Sheffield S7 1SQ
(0114) 2585971
Visitors welcome by appointment only

Patrick Sargent
Glaserberg
3453 Heimisbach
Switzerland
(00 41) 34 712244
Visitors welcome by prior arrangement. Students with genuine interest in wood firing are often accepted for short periods

Micki Schloessingk
Bridge
Cheriton
Gower
W. Glamorgan SA3 1BY
(01792) 386279
Visitors are very welcome to workshop but please telephone first

David Scott
33 Cross Lane
Mountsorrel
Leics. LE12 7BU
(0116) 2302100
Visitors welcome by appointment

Ray Silverman
35 Dunster Crescent
Hornchurch
Essex RM11 3QD
(01708) 458864
Visitors by appointment

Michael Skipwith
Lotus Pottery
Stoke Gabriel
Totnes
S. Devon TQ9 6SL
(01803) 782 303
Workshop and showroom open Monday to Friday 9.00am-5.30pm and usually on Saturday mornings 9.00am-1.00pm

Peter Smith
Higher Bojewyan
Pendeen
Penzance
Cornwall TR19 7TR
(01736) 788820
Visitors welcome

John Solly
Goldspur Cottage
Flackley Ash
Peasmarsh
Rye
East Sussex TN31 6YH
(01797) 230 276
The pottery is opposite the Flackley Ash Hotel on the A268. Visitors are welcome at any time, but if coming from afar, please telephone first

Peter Stoodley
Little Rings
Buckland Rings
Sway Road
Lymington
Hampshire SO41 8NN
(01590) 679778
Visitors welcome by appointment

Harry Horlock Stringer
Taggs Yard
23 Woodlands Road
Barnes
London SW13 0JZ
(0181) 876 5750
Visits arranged by telephone appointments only

Helen Swain
8 Fyfield Road
Waltham Forest
London E17 3RG
(0181) 520 4043
This is a one-person pottery, so visitors by appointment and, sorry, no students possible

Sutton Taylor
Ravenstones
Mount Pleasant North
Robin Hoods Bay
nr Whitby
North Yorkshire YO22 4RE
(01947) 880614
Workshop open to visitors by appointment

Sabina Teuteberg
86 Cecilia Road
London E8 2ET
(0171) 241 5279
Visitors welcome, but by appointment only

Owen Thorpe
Churchstoke Pottery
Old School
Castle Street
Churchstoke
Powys SY15 6AG
(01588) 620 511   (01938) 561 618
Open 9.30am - 2.00pm Other times by appointment

Vera Tollow
Delmonden Oasthouse
Horns Hill
Hawkhurst
Kent TN18 4XD
(01580) 752270
Visitors welcome by appointment

Marianne de Trey
The Cabin
Shinners Bridge
Dartington, Totnes
Devon TQ9 6JB
(01803) 862046 (after 6pm)
Visitors preferably by appointment

Judy Trim
3 Coningham Mews
London W12 9QW
(0181) 749 1190
Occasional visitors by appointment only

Ruthanne Tudball
Norfolk House
344 Wokingham Road
Earley, Reading
Berks. RG6 2DE
(01734) 268003
I have no showroom but visitors are welcome to the
workshop by appointment only

Tina Vlassopulos
29 Canfield Gardens
London NW6 3JP
Tel. (0171) 624 4582   Fax.(0171) 328 1483
Visitors by appointment

Josie Walter
Pottery Workshop
via Gellia Mill
Bonsall
Derbyshire DE4 2AJ
(01629) 825178
Visitors always welcome. Please telephone to check
we are there

John Ward
Fachongle Uchaf
Cilgwyn
Newport
Dyfed SA42 0QR
(01239) 820 706
Visitors by appointment

Sasha Wardell
Le Peyroux
Chabrignac
19350 Juillac
France
(00 33) 55 25 61 10
Visitors welcome by appointment

Robin Welch
Robin Welch Pottery
Stradbroke
Eye
Suffolk IP21 5JP
(01379384) 416
Open 9.00am-6.00pm everyday

John Wheeldon
18 Oakerthorpe Road
Bolehill
Derbyshire DE4 4GP
(01629) 822356
No showroom; visitors are very welcome but please
telephone first

David White
4 Callis Court Road
Broadstairs
Kent CT10 3AE
(01843) 863145
No showroom, but please telephone

Mary White
Zimmerplatzweg 6
55599 Wonsheim
Germany
06703/2922

Visitors welcome, but please telephone first

Caroline Whyman
21 Iliffe Yard
Crampton Street
London SE17 3QA
(0171) 708 5904

Workshop open only by appointment, please
telephone first

David Winkley
Vellow Pottery
Lower Vellow
Williton
Taunton
Somerset TA4 4LS
(01984) 56458

Workshop and pottery open to visitors from 8.30am
until 6.00pm Monday to Saturday

Mollie Winterburn
Tan Cnwch
Ystrad Meurig
Dyfed SY25 6AB
(01874) 831 275

Mary Wondrausch
The Pottery
Brickfields
Compton
nr Guildford
Surrey GU3 1HZ
(01483) 414097

Mon-Fri. 9.00am-5.00pm; Sat and Sun 2.00-5.00pm

Gary Wood
2 Avonvale Place
Batheaston
Bath
Avon BA1 7RF

Steve Woodhead
65 Shakespeare Gardens
Rugby
Warwickshire CV22 6HA
(01788) 522178

Visitors welcome, but please telephone first

**Rosemary D Wren ARCA and
Peter M Crotty**
The Oxshott Pottery
Nutwood Steading
Strathpeffer
Ross & Cromartie IV14 9DT
(01997) 421 478

Visitors are welcome but please telephone first.
Strathpeffer - a Victorian spa - is on the central
Highland east-west road A834, 20 miles NW of
Inverness. Take the M9/A9 from Stirling and turn off
through Dingwall (thus avoiding Strathpeffer by-pass).
The Nutwood drive is on the right just before the 30
mph sign. From London by road is 571 miles; or
coming up to the Highlands in 1½ hours by air
Heathrow/Inverness can cost less than the 13 hour
train journey

Muriel P Wright
Ashanwell
Potkins Lane
Orford, Woodbridge
Suffolk IP12 2SS
(01394) 450580

Oxidised stoneware, glazed white with blue
decoration. Lamps, bowls, dishes and fountain bowls.
Trained at Manchester College of Art. Potting for over
30 years. Founder member of CPA. Visitors welcome
but telephone call essential

Takeshi Yasuda
37 Kensington Gardens
Bath BA1 6LH
Tel: (01225) 334 136   Fax: (01225) 313 492

Workshop open to public by appointment

Joanna and Andrew Young
A & J Young Pottery
Common Farm
Sustead Road
Lower Gresham
Norfolk NR11 8RE
(01263) 577 548

Small shop open at Common Farm every weekday.
For weekend opening times and directions please
telephone

Addresses of Professionals

Billy Adams
39 Cosmeston Street
Cathays
Cardiff
CF2 4LQ
(01222) 668998
Visitors welcome but please telephone first

Marilyn Andreetti
Belle Vue
16 Gews Corner
Cheshunt
Herts EN8 9BX
(01992) 639969
Visitors welcome but please telephone first

Elizabeth Aylmer
Widgery House
20 Market Street
Hatherleigh
Devon EX20 3JP
(01837) 810624
Shop and Showroom open daily, but please telephone
out of season

Sylph Baier
Tin Star Studio
38 Cheltenham Place
Brighton
Sussex BN1 4AB
(01273) 682042
Visitors are welcome by appointment

Chris Barnes
Farleigh Studios
Farleigh Place
Stoke Newington
London N16 7SX
Visitors are welcome, best to ring first on
(0171) 226 0235 (evening)

Richard Baxter
Old Leigh Studios
61 High Street
Leigh-on-Sea
Essex SS9 2EP
(01702) 470490
Open Tuesday-Sunday 11am-5pm Closed Monday

John Bedding
8 Tregenna Hill
St. Ives
Cornwall TR26 1JT
(01736) 796324
Visitors welcome, please telephone first

Julian Bellmont
High Street Pottery
24 High Street
Kintbury
Newbury
Berkshire RG15 0TW
(01488) 657388
Visitors welcome Tuesday - Saturday 9am-5.30pm

Kochevet Ben-David
10A Barforth Road
Nunhead
London SE15 3PS
(0171) 732 2984
Visitors welcome, please telephone first

Suzanne Bergne
66 Barkston Gardens
London SW5 0EL
(0171) 373 0668
Visitors are welcome to see work in London or at the
studio. Please make a prior appointment

John Berry
45 Chancery Lane
Beckenham
Kent BR3 2NR
(0181) 658 0351

Gillian Bliss
32 Talbot Street
Canton
Cardiff CF1 9BW
(01222) 373626
Visitors by appointment only please

Keith Booth
100 King Edward Road
Maidstone
Kent ME15 6PL
(01622) 683816
Visitors by appointment only

Richard Boswell
The Malthouse
Bridgefoot Path
Emsworth
Hampshire PO10 7EB

(01329) 284701

Visitors welcome. Advisable to telephone previous evening

David Brown
Highway Cottage
Church Street
Merriott
Somerset

(01460) 75655

Visitors welcome by appointment

Jenny Browne
Shaftesbury Studios
47 Tyneham Road
London SW11 5XH

(0171) 228 0804

Visitors by appointment please

Susan Bruce
4 Pinewood
Woodbridge
Suffolk IP12 4DS

(01394) 384865

Visitors welcome but telephone first

Karen Bunting
53 Beck Road
London E8 4RE

(0171) 249 3016

Visitors welcome by appointment

Jan Bunyan
4 Bridge Road
Butlers Marston
Warwick CV35 0NE

(01926) 641560

Small showroom: Visitors welcome but advisable to telephone first

Kyra Cane
41 Westhill Drive
Mansfield
Nottinghamshire NG18 1PL

(01623) 20815

Visitors welcome telephone first

Tony Carter
Low Road
Debenham
Stowmarket
Suffolk IP14 6QU

(01728) 860475

Pottery and Shop open to public all year round

Trevor Chaplin
Marridge Hill Cottage
Ramsbury
Marlborough
Wiltshire SN8 2HG

(01672) 20486

Visitors welcome but please telephone first

Ian Chapman
17 Poplar Grove
Sale
Cheshire M33 3AX

(0161) 969 9816

Visitors welcome but telephone first

Desmond Clover
Clover Pottery
5 Oldhurst Road
Pidley
Huntingdon
Cambs PE17 3BY

(01487) 841 026

Shop open most days, if travelling any distance, please telephone first

Rosemary Cochrane
Pen-y-Stair Farm
Mamhilad
Pontypool
Gwent NP4 8RG

(01873) 880696

Visitors welcome but please telephone first

Elaine Coles
Elaine Coles Ceramics
Country Gardens Garden Centre
London Road
Windlesham
Surrey GU20 6LL

(01276) 857369

Open Wednesday - Sunday 10am-5pm Visitors welcome

Jo Connell
Witherley Lodge
12 Watling Street
Witherley
Atherstone
Warwickshire CV9 1RD
(01827) 712128
Visitors welcome by appointment

Molly Curley
32 South Rise
Llanishen
Cardiff CF4 5RH
(01222) 756428
Visitors are welcome by appointment

Louise Darby
Clay Barn
Redhill
Alcester
Warwickshire B49 6NQ
(01789) 765214
Visitors welcome but please telephone first for
directions. Some work always on display.

Joyce Davison
Chapel House
75 Pales Green
Castle Acre
King's Lynn
Norfolk PE32 2AL
(01760) 755405
Visitors are welcome but please telephone first if
making special journey

Nick Douglas
34 Fore Street
Bere Alston
Yelverton
Devon PL20 7AD
(01822) 841220
Visitors by appointment

Bridget Drakeford
Upper Buckenhill Farmhouse
Fownhope
Hereford HR1 4PU
(01432) 860411
Visitors welcome by appointment

Victoria and Michael Eden
Parkside
Hale
nr. Milnthorpe
Cumbria LA7 7BL
(015395) 62342

Kirsti Buhler Fattorini
5 Broadway
Hale
Cheshire WA15 0PF
(0161) 980 4504
Visitors by appointment

Judith Fisher
Huntswood
St. Helena's Lane
Streat
nr. Hassocks
Sussex BN6 8SD
(01273) 890088
Visitors by appointment

Hilary Flexon
31 Bathurst Road
Cirencester
Glos. GL7 1SA

Susan Ford
29 Hilltop Road
Ferndown
Dorset BH22 9QT
(01202) 876559
Visitors welcome. Please telephone for appointment

Geraldine Fox
83 Green Lane
Coventry
West Midlands CV3 6DN
(01203) 690244
Visitors by appointment

Liz Gale
Taplands Farm Cottage
Webbs Green
High Street
Soberton
Hampshire SO32 3PY
(01705) 632686
Visitors welcome but please telephone first

Philip Gardiner
8 Fore Street
Mevagissey
Cornwall PL26 6UQ
(01726) 842042

The pottery/shop is in the centre of Mevagissy. Open daily from Easter to Christmas

Rodney George
The Garden House
Thames Road
Goring-on-Thames
Reading
Berks. RG8 9AH
(01491) 873276

Visitors are welcome. Please phone to make sure I am home

Graham Glynn
The Showroom
Howgill Lane
Sedbergh
Cumbria LA10 5DE
(015396) 21586

Visitors by appointment

Paul Green
Abbey Pottery
Cerne Abbas
Dorchester
Dorset DT2 7JQ
(01300) 341865

Customers always welcome.
Showroom open 7 days a week 10am - 6pm.
Closed some Mondays in winter so please phone.

Mark Griffiths
The Old School
Culmington
Ludlow
Shropshire SY8 2DF
(01584) 73212

Visitors welcome, please telephone first

Dimitra Grivellis
Unit 9
Metropolitan Workshops
Enfield Road
London N1 5AZ
(0171) 249 5455

Visitors welcome but please telephone first

Morgen Hall
Studio 5
Chapter Arts Centre
Market Road
Canton
Cardiff CF5 1QE
(01222) 396061 ext.219
(01222) 238716

Visitors always welcome, but please telephone first

Janet Halligan
Oak Bank Farm
Wybunbury Road
Willaston
Nantwich
Cheshire CW5 7ER
(01270) 665703

Visitors welcome but please telephone first

Michael and Barbara Hawkins
The Pottery
Rooksmoor Mills
Bath Road
Stroud
Glos. GL5 5ND
(01453) 873322

Showroom is open 7 days a week 10-4.
All visitors welcome

Christopher Helson
Orchardton House
Auchencairn
Castle Douglas
Dumfries & Galloway DG7 1QL
(01522) 751380

Visitors welcome by appointment

André Hess
32 Seaman Close
St. Albans
Hertfordshire AL2 2NX
(01727) 874299

Visitors welcome but please telephone first

Elaine Hewitt
Summerhill Cottage
Summerhill Lane
Frensham
Surrey GU10 3EN
(01252) 793955

Visitors welcome but telephone first

Andrew Hill
Lower Beardshaw Head
Trawden
Colne
Lancashire BB8 8PP
(01282) 866771
Visitors welcome please telephone first

Anthony B. Hodge
Skyfield Studio
Bennetts Hill
South Littleton
nr. Evesham
Worcs. WR11 5TH
(01386) 832404
Visitors welcome but please telephone first

Terri Holman
The Rainbow Pottery
Rainbow
Avenue Road
Torquay TQ2 5TG
(01803) 295277
Visitors welcome, please telephone first

Paul Jackson
Helland Bridge Pottery
Helland Bridge
Bodmin
Cornwall
(01208) 75240
Visitors welcome, please telephone first

Eileen Jones
Chapelgate Pottery
Chittlehamholt
nr. Umberleigh
Devon EX37 9NS
(01769) 540 538
Open to the public every day except Wednesday
from Easter to end September. By appointment during
winter.

Vresh David Kanikanian
Gallery Tavid
56 St. Mary's Road
London W5 5EX
(0181) 566 1494
Visitors welcome, but please telephone first

Jonathan Keep
JK Pottery
31 Leiston Road
Knodishall
Saxmundham
Suffolk IP17 1UQ
(01728) 832901
Visitors welcome at showroom and workshop
Monday to Saturday 9.30am - 5.30pm

Judith King
Cobbler Cottage
34 Hickleton Village
nr. Doncaster
South Yorkshire DN5 7BG
Tel/Fax (01709) 892848
Visitors welcome by appointment only please

Julian King-Salter
Bancau
Brynberian
Crymych
Dyfed SA41 3TS
(01239) 79 652
Ring or write for showroom opening times, or to
make appointment

Gaynor Lindsell
Whalebones
Wood Street
Barnet
Herts. EN5 4BZ
(0181) 449 5288

Christine McCole
Hafod Hill Pottery
Llanboidy
Whitland
Dyfed SA34 0ER
(01994) 448361
Visitors welcome

Vinitha McWhinnie
22 Widney Manor Road
Solihull
West Midlands B91 3JQ
(0121) 705 8842

Unit 1/133 Custard Factory
Gibb Street
Digbeth
Birmingham B9 4AA
(0121) 604 7777 (messages)
Visitors welcome by appointment

Martin McWilliam
Auf dem Kötjen 1
26209 Sandhatten
Germany
04482/83 72

Made in Cley
Cley next the Sea
Norfolk NR25 7RF
(01263) 740134
Gallery open all year

Fenella Mallalieu
100 Mortimer Road
London N1 4LA
(0171) 241 6553

Angela Mellor
5 Stulpfield Road
Grantchester
Cambridge CB3 9NL
(01223) 840528
Visitors by appointment

Kate Mellors
Rosemead
Marshwood
nr. Bridport
Dorset DT6 5QB
(01297) 678217
Visitors welcome but please telephone first

Toff Milway
Conderton Pottery
The Old Forge
Conderton
nr. Tewkesbury
Glos. GL20 7PP
(01386) 725387
Workshop and showroom open Monday to
Saturday 9am - 5.30pm. Always large selection of
work on display

Jill Moger
The Studio
75 Millfield Lane
Nether Poppleton
York YO2 6NA
(01904) 794874
Studio visits by appointment

Sarah Monk
Bronsil Lodge
Eastnor
Ledbury
Herefordshire HR8 1EP
(01531) 633255
Visitors welcome by appointment

Roger Mulley
Clanfield Pottery
131 Chalton Lane
Clanfield
Waterlooville
Hampshire PO8 0RG
(01705) 595144
Visitors always welcome at weekends

John Mullin
September House
Parnacott
Wolsworthy
Devon EX22 7JD
(01409) 253589

Sue Munday
The Workshop
53 Anderson Avenue
Earley
Reading
Berkshire RG6 1HD
(01734) 265063

Stephen Murfitt
The Workshop
18 Stretham Road
Wicken
Cambs. CB7 5XH
(01353) 721160
Visitors welcome by appointment

Tessa Wolfe Murray
2 Spenser Road
London SE24 0NR
(0171) 733 9822
Visitors welcome by appointment

Christine Niblett
Sa Cantera
Calle Pastoritx 2
Son Vida
07013 Palma de Mallorca
Spain
(71) 791787
Only 10 minutes from centre of Palma. Visitors
welcome but best telephone first

Jacqueline Norris
81 High Street
Eton
Windsor
Berks. SL4 6AF

(01753) 860771

Visitors welcome to gallery at any time, studio visits by appointment

Carol Peevor
76 Park Lane
Wednesbury
West Midlands WS10 9PT

(0121) 556 0247

Visitors (occasional) by appointment please

Rebecca Peters
Sopwell Mill Farm
Cottonmill Lane
St. Albans
Herts. AL1 2ES

(01727) 853285

Studio open Spring 1995 - visitors welcome by appointment only

Nancy Pickard
c/o Contemporary Ceramics
7, Marshall Street
London W1V 1LP

Philomena Pretsell
Rose Cottage
10 Fountain Place
Loanhead
Midlothian EH20 9EA

(0131) 440 0751

Workshop at home, 5 miles from Edinburgh, with visitors welcome by appointment

Ursula Morley Price
Chez Gaty
Vaux Lavalette
16320 Villebois
France

Tel. 45 259167

Gaynor Reeve
Callis Court
London Road
West Malling
Kent ME19 5AH

Audrey Richardson
Morawel
Parrog Road
Newport
Pembrokeshire SA42 0RF

(01239) 820 449

Visitors welcome by appointment

Margaret Rollason
19 Oakside Close
Evington
Leicester LE5 6SN

(0116) 2 412188

Visitors welcome, please telephone first

Michael and Wendy Salt
Aislaby Pottery
Aislaby
Pickering
North Yorkshire YO18 8PE

(01751) 474128

Showroom open most days 10am-5pm

Nicolette Savage
145 Goodhart Way
West Wickham
Kent BR4 0EU

(0181) 777 8372

Caroline Seaton
Amberley Village Pottery
Church Street
Amberley
nr. Arundel
West Sussex

(01798) 831876

Open most days, all year, 11am-5.30pm in summer and 11am-4pm winter.

Wim Seelde
6 Bute Street
Brighton BN2 2EH

Sheila Seepersaud-Jones
5 Brookland Rise
London NW11 6DN

Ifigenija Simonovic´
21 Crownhill Road
Woodford Bridge
Essex IG8 8JF

(0181) 505 7679

Graham Skinner
Studio One
1 Victoria Street
Rochester
Kent ME1 1XJ
(01634) 811469
Visitors welcome by appointment

Charles Spacey
Pant-y-Ddafad
Pont Robert
Meifod
Powys SY22 6JF
(01938) 500 620
Visitors welcome but please telephone first

Peter Sparrey
90 Worcester Road
Link Top
Malvern
Worcestershire WR14 1NY
(01684) 577173

Chris Speyer
Yerja Ceramics & Textiles
Mill Rise
Ford Road
Bampton
Devon EX16 9LW
(01398) 331163
Visitors welcome but telephone first

Christel Spriet
The Hermitage
35 College Road
Framlingham
Suffolk IP13 9ER
(01728) 724333
Studio open by appointment

TAJA
Pottery House
38 Cross Street
Moretonhampstead
Devon TQ13 8NL

Rebecca Taylor
18 Clarion House
St. Anne's Court
Soho
London W1V 3AX
(0171) 434 2924

Lyndon Thomas
Swn y Môr
Llanarth
Aberaeron
Dyfed SA47 0PZ
(01545) 580406
Visitors welcome by appointment

Katrina Trinick
Lesquite
Lanivet
Bodmin
Cornwall PL30 5HT
(01208) 831716
Visitors welcome but please telephone first

Clare Parsons Trucco
107 Marchmont Road
Edinburgh EH9 1HA
(0131) 447 2424
Visitors welcome but please telephone first

Tydd Pottery
Pode Hole
Spalding
Lincs. PE11 3QA
(01775) 766120

Sue Varley
54 Elthorne Road
Uxbridge
Middlesex UB8 2PS
(01895) 231738
Visitors welcome but please telephone

Carol Wainwright
Little Durnford
Old Malthouse Lane
Langton Matravers
Dorset BH19 3HH
(01929) 425905
Visitors by appointment

Andrew Watts
Lannock Pottery
Weston Barns
Hitchin Road
Weston
Hitchin
Herts. SG4 7AX
Tel. (01462) 790356   Fax. (01462) 790704
Shop open Monday-Saturday 10-5pm
Sunday 11-5pm. Visitors welcome to workshop.

Jenny Welch
High House
Stradbroke
Eye
Suffolk IP21 5JP

Nicola Werner
The Old Parsonage
Hemyock
nr. Cullompton
Devon EX15 3RG
(01823) 680957
Visitors welcome but by appointment only

David Constantine White
Briar Hey Pottery
Burnley Road
Mytholmroyd
West Yorkshire HX7 5PG
(01422) 885725
Open usual trading hours

George Wilson
48B Mulgrave Road
Ealing
London W5 1LE
(0181) 998 4470
Visitors welcome by appointment

Brigitte Winsor
145A Lower High Street
The Harlequin Centre
Watford
Herts WD1 2TA

Karen Ann Wood
3 Foxgrove Avenue
Beckenham
Kent BR3 2BA
(0181) 658 2759
Visitors welcome but should telephone beforehand

Gill Wright
52 South Street
Epsom
Surrey KT18 7PQ
(01372) 723908
Visitors very welcome but please telephone for appointment first

Becoming A Potter

Ceramic Opportunities in the United Kingdom

The opportunities for studying ceramics are many and varied, ranging from full-time and part-time courses in art departments in colleges of further education, universities, part-time courses at local institutes, weekends with well-known potters to teaching yourself from books and videos. In this section the various possibilities are detailed under different headings.

Courses

Many well-established potters offer short courses aimed either at the beginner or the more experienced maker. These may be for one day to two weeks or more. Many of these courses are listed in each issue of *Ceramic Review* and most will supply a brochure outlining what is offered. It is often useful to ask to speak to people who have been on the course if you want a user's view.

Videos and Films

Many videos and films of potters at work are available. They are a good guide to the working methods of individual potters, though no real substitute for a good teacher who can answer questions and deal with your particular need. However, they are excellent as back-up material. A free list of available videos and films on craft and design (including ceramics) can be obtained from the Crafts Council, 44a Pentonville Road, London N1 9BY.

Part-time Courses

Many BA (Hons) courses are now open to part-time students. In addition local education authorities offer a wide range of part-time courses. Some are classed as 'Non-vocational' but many have been set up to give a first-class education so that, over a period of time, they provide a thorough training in studio pottery techniques. Many Art Colleges, Technical Colleges and Colleges of Adult and Further Education (including some of the ones listed here) offer such courses, some giving their own certificate of proficiency. As the intake is irregular and the age and standard of students variable it is usual for each student to follow his/her own course of indefinite duration. Particulars of these and evening institutes in the area can be obtained from your local Adult Education Centre or from the Chief Education Officer of your Education Authority.

Local education authorities also provide evening and day part-time courses for beginners and for more advanced students. Classes last approximately two hours. Fees are relatively modest and concessions may be offered for people out of work. Basic materials are provided and finished work can be purchased at a minimal cost. Personal tools are not usually supplied. Instructors vary in skill and teaching ability and it is worth asking other students how they have fared. Full information on available classes can be obtained from your local Public Library or Education Office. In London the booklet Floodlight lists all currently available classes and can be obtained through most newsagents and bookshops. New sessions start in September each year. It is worth remembering that pottery classes are usually very popular so book early. However, some vacant places occur during the year which can be taken up by new students.

Workshop Training

Because of the very diverse nature of studio pottery few formal apprenticeship schemes exist for training prospective potters at present, though with the introduction of National Vocational Qualifications (NVQs) by the government some nationally recognised basis will be set up. The kind of work undertaken by trainees, and the amount and quality of the teaching they receive in the studio of the individual potter will depend largely on the skill and outlook of the potter they work for, and the agreement that is made. While few potters will, or are able to, offer a full-time, two-year training, many will take an assistant for a few days or weeks for specific projects.

Joining a workshop requires determination and a degree of luck. The number of potters employing assistants is small, demand for places often exceeds supply, and competition is, therefore, fierce. Success in finding a potter to work with whose pots you admire will require commitment, strong perseverance and almost certainly some measure of being in the right place at the right time.

You can try to join a pottery direct as a trainee assistant with little or no previous experience, or for a period of workshop practice following an art school ceramics course. One with a strong bias towards studio pottery would be an advantage.

The work of some potters is so individual that it almost precludes additional help. Those who do employ assistants often spend much of their time making repetition ware, decorative or functional. Students leaving art schools for workshops may find the change constricting and it is best to bear this in mind. Much of the learning will inevitably be done by making pots designed initially by the potters and the opportunities for personal expression are likely to be limited.

There are no standard rates of pay for trainees and remuneration will be set according to their means in relation to the real productive help that an assistant can give. It is the experience of many potters that assistants often over-estimate their ability to make pots quickly and of a saleable quality. Some potters regard the training as payment. The Crafts Council offer a variety of Training Grant Schemes. Some are intended for established craftworkers and these are a great help in supplementing the wages of trainees. But this scheme is not automatically available to every potter with assistants and it must be assumed that the rate of pay for trainees will be less - and in some cases considerably less - than those in industry or teaching.

The names and addresses of Fellows and Professional Members of the Craft Potters Association are listed in this book. Many other potters are included in 'Visiting Craft Workshops' published by the Rural Development Commission. A list of potters who work with assistants can be obtained from the Crafts Council. Regional Art Boards usually have a Craft Officer who can give useful advice on opportunities available in the area.

Application to Studios

Before applying to a potter try to see the work of as many potters as you can so that you are clear about the kind of pots you want to make. If, for example, your main interest is ceramic sculpture you are likely to be happier working with a potter whose prime interest this is than one preoccupied with domestic ware. Just writing a letter which says, in essence, 'I am interested in pottery. Do you have a job?' is unlikely to gain a positive response. Potters get many such letters from applicants who appear to post a dozen or so at a time to widely differing potters in the hope that something will turn up.

The better, and probably only, way is to go and see the potters of your choice in their studios. This requires a lot of effort, it is time-consuming and demands perseverance mentioned earlier. But in seeking a workshop place you are, in effect, asking potters to make a commitment to you in time, energy and money. Potters have livings to earn and they must be as sure as they can that you are really serious about working with them to mutual advantage. In short they have to be convinced that there is something in it for them as well as you.

Before you visit, telephone or write to see that it is convenient. Take with you any examples or photographs of pots you have made. Without some evidence it is very difficult for potters to judge an applicant's ability or potential.

Working successfully and harmoniously as a member of a small team, or in conjunction with an individual potter, is as much a question of good personal relationships as the teaching and acquisition of skills. In the search for workshop places, therefore, it is difficult to over- estimate the value of personal contact. This works both ways: it enables potters to judge at first hand an applicant's response to the work they do and, equally important, it gives applicants the opportunity to see what facilities are available and to say what they can offer the workshop. Trainees have much to give in enthusiasm for and commitment to working with clay, and in ready willingness to share all the many and sometimes tedious jobs that every workshop has to undertake to produce finished pots.

Courses in art colleges, polytechnics and universities

Graduate level courses BA (Hons)

These three or four year Courses (full-time) preceded by a one or two year Foundation Course aim for the development of the individual rather than his/her training for a specific employment situation. Entry is highly competitive and educational requirements stringent (usually 5 GCE 'O' level passes or GCSEs although some colleges demand one or two 'A' level passes). Pottery (Ceramics) is usually contained in three dimensional design, and courses may include work in other media and Art History and Complementary Studies. In the Colleges offering Ceramics as a chief study the emphasis varies between craft, fine-art and industrial design pottery. Intending students should study prospectuses or visit courses before making application.

For residents in the UK grants for these courses are mandatory, once a place has been secured, but are subject to means tests and other certain conditions. Overseas students usually have to pay full fees.

Vocational courses and BTEC

These courses differ from the above in these respects

- Entry requirements are usually less stringent.

- Courses are geared more towards professional training for subsequent employment as a technician, craftworker, designer/craftworker or designer.

- Grants are at the discretion of the LEAs.

- Courses vary from 2 - 4 years.

- Courses, which usually lead to a local, regional or professional Diploma or Licentiateship include some ancillary studies in drawing, design and other craft techniques.

No official 'sandwich' courses for studio potters exist at present but some colleges make informal arrangements for students to work in potters' workshops during the course or in vacations.

Colleges offering courses in ceramics

College	Course, entry requirements & qualifications and description of course supplied by college
ENGLAND	
Alsager	
Crewe & Alsager Faculty The Manchester Metropolitan University Hassall Road Alsager Staffs. ST7 2HL Tel: (0161) 247 5302 Fax: (0161) 247 6377	**BA (Hons) Crafts** Combined Studies: Wood/Metal/Ceramics/Textiles. Course description:The course gives a grounding in each of the four materials during the first half-year, after which students select two for continuing combined exploration. This encourages unusual and inventive approaches to media and techniques. Visual and historical research are integral, complementary elements of the degree. Also included in the course are a dissertation and a Business Unit dealing with both basic skills and a small business planning project.
Amersham	
Amersham & Wycombe College Stanley Hill Amersham Bucks HP7 9HN Tel: (01494) 735555 Fax: (01494) 735566	Ceramics included as an element in our Art Foundation course, **BTEC General Art** & Design course 'A' Level Ceramics - entry GCSE in Art or Ceramics together with portfolio of art and design Evening classes in Pottery These courses act as feeders to courses of higher education namely HND or B.A. in Ceramics or associate subjects. Part-time courses (11 weeks) starting January, April and September.
Bath	
Bath College of Higher Education Faculty of Art and music Sion Hill Place Lansdown Bath BA1 5SF Tel: (01225) 425254 Fax: (01225) 445228	**BA (Hons) Ceramics** The course is designed to equip students with an understanding of contemporary ceramics and an education in the broad range of approaches, techniques, craft skills and industrial processes. Supporting studies offer options to work in other mediums and Complementary Studies develop analytical and critical skills, placing Art and Design activities amongst the other cultural, historical and social practices.

Birmingham	**Birmingham Institute of Art and Design** University of Central England Corporation Street Birmingham B4 7DX Tel: (0121) 331 5819/5820	**BA (Hons) Three Dimensional Design Ceramics with Glass** 1 year foundation course or equivalent 5 GCSEs 18+ Minimum
Bradford	**Bradford & Ilkley Community College** School of Art Design & Textiles Great Horton Road Bradford West Yorkshire BD7 1AY Tel: (01274) 753240	**BTEC National Diploma in Design Crafts** (with Ceramics Strand). Full or part-time study available. The ceramics strand is broadly based and the pursuit of individual interests and concerns is encouraged. We have a wide range of National level courses which can lead on to degree level study - including Bradford **BA (Hons) Art & Design**. A course which allows students to interrelate media areas across Art and/or Design. Students may combine Ceramics with one of the following: Painting, Illustration, Graphics, Textiles or Printmaking.
Brighton	**University of Brighton** Faculty of Art Design and Humanities Grand Parade Brighton BN2 2JY Tel: (01273) 643081 Fax: (01273) 643055	**BA (Hons) Wood Metal Ceramics Plastics course**. 3 years full-time. Normally 1-year foundation + 5 'O' levels or 2 'A' and 3 'O' levels. Direct entry in exceptional circumstances. Folio interview, ADAR application or University application for overseas students. The course is concerned with the work of the artist-craftsperson and designer-maker working within material areas or across them. A minimum of two material areas must be taken in years 1 and 2. Idea development, design and visual research are carried through in self-directed project work in three dimensions. Written work in Art and Design History is 20% or more of the degree.
Bristol	**UWE Bristol** Faculty of Art, Media & Design Clanage Road, Bower Ashton Bristol BS3 2JU Tel: (0117) 9660222 × 4759	**BA (Hons) Ceramics.** The course provides a broad experience of ceramics; established techniques are studied forming the basis for independent development. Ceramics is part of the faculty wide modular scheme which enables students to take part in an extensive range of practical and theoretical art and design studies. The modules are designed to stimulate interest not only in the intrinsic and expressive qualities of ceramics but also in the exciting areas where complementary disciplines overlap. The final year centres on individual, self-directed, programmes of work.

Carlisle

Cumbria College of Art & Design
Brampton Road
Carlisle
Cumbria CA3 9AY
Tel: (01228) 25333
Fax: (01228) 514491

BTEC Design (Crafts) Successful applicants initially select Textiles or Ceramics as their Craft Study Option. Textiles includes Fabric Printing, Multi-Media Textiles and Ceramics includes: Throwing, Press Moulding, Handbuilding, Slip Casting, Glaze Technology. In addition all students will undertake supporting options which may be used in conjunction with their main craft area in the manufacture of a wide range products. Visual studies and Contextual Studies support all areas and considerable emphasis is given to Business Awareness.
BA (Hons) in Design Crafts This is a multi-disciplinary course providing students with the opportunity to study ceramics with multi-media textiles and printed textiles. The practical craft options are supported by units in Design History, Cultural Studies, Visual Research and Design Development and Professional Practice and Business Awareness.

Derby

University of Derby
Kedleston Road
Derby DE3 1GB
Tel: (01332) 347181
Fax: (01332) 294861

BTEC Higher National Diploma in Design (Crafts) Studio Ceramics
Entry requirements: BTEC Diploma in General Vocational Design or General Art and Design or the satisfactory completion of a Foundation Course or a course of an equivalent level or mature students with appropriate experience or students transferring at the end of first year of BA course in Ceramics or appropriate industrial experience or, exceptionally, sixth form 'A' level candidates.

Eastbourne

College of Arts & Technology
Eversley Court
St. Anne's Road
Eastbourne
Sussex BN21 2HS
Tel: (01323) 644711

One-year Foundation. 2-year BTEC GNVQ General art and design: ceramics specialist design option. City and Guilds 2-year part-time diploma in creative ceramic studies.

Exeter

Exeter Faculty of Art and Design
University of Plymouth
Earl Richards Road North
Exeter EX2 6AS
Tel: (01392) 412211

BA (Hons) Design (3 Dimensional Design)
BA (Hons) Fine Art

Falmouth

Falmouth College of Arts
Woodlane
Falmouth
Cornwall TR11 4RA
Tel: (01326) 211077
Fax: (01326) 211205

BA (Hons) Degree Studio Ceramics
Course content: Visual Studies: Drawing from the environment and the Figure; Design Methodologies; Contextual Studies; Art, Design and Ceramic History; Production Studies; Wheel Work; Hand-forming; Mould-making; Technical Studies; Clay and Glaze; Formulation; Ceramic Chemistry; Firing Strategies; Professional Studies; Health and Safety; Career Development. Further opportunities: Self employment; community work; employment; post-graduate study in ceramics; mural design; art therapy; arts administration; art restoration; teaching, etc.

Farnham	**West Surrey College of Art and Design**

Falkner Road
Farnham
Surrey GU9 7DS
Tel: (01252) 722441
Fax: (01252) 733869

BA (Hons) 3DD Ceramics
5 GCSEs Grade C or above. Applicants normally will have successfully completed a Foundation Course or BTEC National Diploma. Ceramics is part of the BA (Hons) Three Dimensional Design which embraces Glass and Metals in the Faculty of Design. The programme offers a stimulating and challenging opportunity to study in exceptionally well equipped studios.

Gloucester **Royal Forest of Dean College**
Five Acres Campus
Coleford
Gloucestershire GL16 7JT
Tel: (01594) 833416

BTEC National Diploma in Design Ceramics A two-year studio ceramics course aimed at students wishing to set up their own workshops or progress to Degree level courses. Students specialise after an introductory programme including a range of production techniques, glazing, kiln building and firing. Supporting studies include drawing and design, contextual and professional studies. Modern purpose-built studios. Applications from mature students welcome. Advisory interviews may be arranged by telephone.

Harrogate **Harrogate College**
Hornbeam Park
Hookstone Road
Harrogate
North Yorkshire HG2 8QT
Tel: (01423) 879466

GNVQ Advanced Programme
Offering Specialist Pathway in Ceramic Design with opportunities to progress to H.E. or employment. Accreditation for prior learning will be considered for mature students. Course includes introductions to handbuilding, throwing, modelling, mouldmaking and industrial techniques, clay and glaze technology, kiln building (Raku, wood and salt firings) leading to individual specialist involvement in aspects of these practical studies, a Visual Studies programme which includes drawing and colour studies, design studies, surface design and photography; Historical and Contextual Studies together with aspects of Business Studies.

Hereford **Herefordshire College of Art and Design**
Folly Lane
Hereford HR1 1LT
Tel: (01432) 273359
Fax: (01432) 341099

BTEC HND Design Crafts: Course that prepares students for entrance into the professional world of the designer/maker. To achieve this objective the prerequisite skills and knowledge required for the successful running of a small business are directly reflected in the course philosophy, content and structure both at a practical and theoretical level. Options in: ceramics, metal, textiles. These are supported by a comprehensive range of media, both traditional and non-traditional. Technical material resource may be combined as appropriate. **City & Guilds of London Institute Creative Studies (7900) Ceramics**. This part-time one day a week course includes a wide range of forming and decorative techniques and is supported by visits to workshops, museums and galleries. Previous experience is not required and the programme is taught over two years with continuous assessment. A core unit 'preparing designs and working drawings' is included in the syllabus. Entry requirements minimum age 16 years. No formal qualifications.

High Wycombe

Buckinghamshire College of Higher Education, a college of Brunel University
Queen Alexandra Road
High Wycombe
HP11 2JZ
Tel: (01494) 522141
Fax: (01494) 524392

BA (Hons) Ceramics with Glass
Applicants must have completed Art Foundation Course and be over 18 with 5 GCSEs or 3 GCSEs and one 'A' level. This exciting course provides a broad-based experience of working with both clay and glass, and students are taught both studio and industrial craft skills. The aim of the course is to help students develop a personal and visual awareness through working with these materials, thus providing a sound basis for their future development as artists and designers.

King's Lynn

Norfolk College of Arts & Technology
Tennyson Avenue
King's Lynn PE30 2QW
Tel: (01553) 761144

BTEC National Diploma in Ceramics
2-year full-time course

Leicester

School of Design and and Manufacture
De Montfort University
The Gateway
Leicester LE1 9BH
(0116) 2577523
(0116) 2577574

BA (Hons) Ceramics/Glass Entry requirements: 5 'O' plus Foundation or BTEC. Does not accept direct entry. Applications from mature students welcome. Each student has the opportunity to work with a variety of media and experience a wide range of attitudes to problem solving. From the very beginning the course is involved with both the practice and theory of design for production as well as the realisation of personal dreams and fantasies. Live projects, and we have a unique record in winning national competitions.

London

Camberwell College of Arts
(The London Institute)
Peckham Road
London SE5 8UF
Tel: (0171) 703 0987
Fax: (0171) 703 3689

BA (Hons) Full-time Course. The course enables students to exploit the medium and to understand and enjoy the versatility of ceramics and the scope it offers for creative thinking, designing and making. The ceramics specialist study is a three-year full-time course leading to the award of a BA Honours Degree. It provides for the designing and making of objects in fired clay, in a craft-based studio/workshop context.

Central Saint Martins College of Art & Design
(The London Institute)
Southampton Row
London WC1B 4AP
Tel: (0171) 753 9090
Fax: (0171) 242 0240

BA (Hons) Ceramic Design The course explores functional ceramic design through a wide range of approaches open to the ceramic designer. It produces graduates with a high level of intellectual maturity that makes them eligible for a number of distinctive careers open to the professional ceramist.

Barnet College
Wood Street
Barnet
Herts. EN5 4AZ
Tel: (0181) 440 6321
Fax: (0181) 441 5236

BTEC GNVQ Advanced in Art and Design Full-time 2-year diagnostic Art and Design 16+ **BTEC National Diploma in Design 3D Studies.** Full-time, wood, ceramics, engineering in application to product design.

Middlesex University
Faculty of Art, Design and
Performing Arts
Cat Hill
Barnet
Herts EN4 8HT
Tel: (0181) 362 5000

BA (Hons) Ceramics The Ceramics modular course offers a full-time 3 or 4 year specialist study. There is a part-time option of 2 days per week for 6 years. Students wishing to do a placement or foreign exchange would complete the course in 4 years. Students will be asked at interview the length of course required. First year modules in ceramics involve learning essential basic skills and methods in handbuilding, throwing and industrial production. Ceramics covers a broad area of activity offering three pathways of study: (1) Industrial Design (2) Craft (3) Sculpture.

University of Westminster Harrow College
Northwick Park
Harrow HA1 3TP
Tel: (0171) 911 5000

3 years Workshop Ceramics BA (Hons) Standard entry with Foundation or BTEC Diploma. Non-standard entry for mature students (21+). The Workshop Ceramics BA(Hons) Course accepts no narrow definitions of Studio pottery but seeks to promote excellence and, by the examination of historical and contemporary practice and through mastery of related craft skills, to extend the conceptual possibilities of the discipline. The particular philosophy that has evolved at Harrow, rooted in the acquisition of a sound understanding of the craft skills and disciplines are an essential foundation for personal research and development, has been well documented and vindicated by the professional successes of its past students.

West Thames College
London Road
Isleworth
Middlesex TW7 4HS
Tel: (0181) 568 0244
Fax: (0181) 569 7787

Foundation Course 1 year, 5 GCSEs or equivalents plus a good portfolio. **BTEC Advanced GNVQ in Art & Design** 2 years, 4 GCSEs or equivalents and a good portfolio.

Loughborough

Loughborough College of Art & Design
Radmoor
Loughborough
Leicester LE11 3BT
Tel: (01509) 261515
Fax: (01509) 265515

BA(Hons) 3-Dimensional Ceramics Entrance qualifications as standard but main criteria for acceptance is portfolio and commitment. As in all Art and Design degrees 20% of the course is taken up with academic work and prospective students should be able to demonstrate an ability to cope with the written work. The course is a 3-year full-time (5-year part-time) specialist degree in ceramics, there are support studies in photography and computers in the structured 1st year, and this leads progressively into self-directed working in the 2nd and 3rd years.

Lowestoft	**School of Art & Design** **Lowestoft College** St Peters Street Lowestoft Suffolk NR32 2NB Tel: (01502) 583521 Fax: (01502) 500031	**BTEC HND in Ceramic Design** 2 years full-time attendance. Requirements: Normally 4 GCSEs at Grade C or above, or equivalent. However, if you are a mature student, or if you can demonstrate some prior knowledge of the subject or have a good portfolio of general art-work which you can present at interview, then we may be able to accept you on to the course with fewer formal qualifications. Practical experience including drawing and visual research, surface pattern design; studio crafts - handbuilding and throwing; industrial ceramics; sculptural ceramics; clay. glaze and kiln technologies; mould-making and kiln building; business and professional studies.
Manchester	**Manchester Metropolitan University** Faculty of Art and Design Department of Three Dimensional Design Chatham Building All Saints Manchester M15 6BR Tel: (0161) 247 1003	**BA (Hons) 3D Design, Wood, Metal, Ceramics, Glass**. This is a multi-disciplinary course where students may choose to specialise in ceramics during their final year. All students work across a wide area of materials. The course in ceramics covers all basic making techniques including throwing, handbuilding and simple mould making. A diverse range of approaches is encouraged in the expressive use of clay. The course is initially project-based and includes relevant glaze and kiln technology together with some historical studies. In the final year students develop their own personal approach to clay.
Middlesbrough	**Cleveland College of Art and Design** Green Lane Middlesbrough Cleveland TS9 6DE Tel: (01642) 821441	**BTEC GNVQ and Foundation Studies** plus NCFE 'Access' course with specialisms in studio ceramics leading to advanced levels
Nuneaton	**North Warwickshire College** Hinckley Road Nuneaton CV11 6BH Tel: (01203) 349321 Fax: (01203) 329056	**BTEC National Diploma in Design Ceramics** Entry by 4 GCSEs and/or portfolio of work demonstrating a commitment to ceramics. A full-time 2-year course designed for students interested in a professional career as a designer/maker/ technician in Ceramics. The aim is to provide students with the skills and knowledge necessary for continued further education or employment, enabling them to follow a career related to their interests and skills in the design studio of a factory, the ceramic workshop or studio pottery.

Preston	**University of Central Lancashire** **Faculty of Design and Technology** Preston PR1 2TQ (01772) 201201	**BA (Hons) Three Dimensional Design Course** The Course offers the opportunity to study three dimensional design work ranging from craft to design manufacture, and offers a broad range of disciplines which can be integrated or studied as specialist activities. We have a firm belief that the individuality of each student should be nurtured and that a multi-faceted course can produce graduates who have highly developed skills and are equipped for life as designer makers intending to satisfy exclusive markets or as designers for industry well versed in problem solving and product development. Course of Study: Initial study units introduce students to the knowledge and skills required for advanced study of specialist options, with projects becoming more student-initiated as the course progresses. With appropriate guidance students plot their own route through the programme.
Rochester	**Kent Institute of Art and Design Rochester-upon-Medway College** Fort Pitt Rochester Kent ME1 1DZ Tel: (01634) 830022	**BA (Hons) Three Dimensional Design: (Pathways in Ceramic Design, Interior Architecture and and Creative Modelmaking)** The ceramics parthway will offer a broad and divergent experience of ceramics, investigating established processes and techniques of craft based and industrial ceramics. Design projects which direct the students' experience towards ceramics within architecture and the built environment, public arts, architectural restoration and product design will form a major part of the 2nd year studies, leading to individual, self-directed programmes of study in Year 3. **National Diploma in Design** Option in Ceramics, 2 years. Entry Requirements: Minimum age 16 years, minimum 3 GCSE/GCE 'O' levels or equivalent plus evidence of art/craft/design study. The course including drawing, painting and designing and complementary studies which encourages interest in the historical, social. economical and philosophical aspects of the craft. All techniques are covered.
Rotherham	**Rotherham College of Arts and Technology** Eastwood Lane Rotherham South Yorks S65 1EG Tel: (01709) 362111	**GCSE and City and Guilds courses** with options through the General Art and Design, Foundation and Access programmes, for people wishing to specialise in Ceramics through a higher education course.
Stafford	**Stafford College** Earl Street Stafford Staffordshire ST16 2QR Tel: (01785) 223800	**City and Guilds Creative Studies, Ceramics,** Ceramic Design and Production

Stoke-on-Trent	**Staffordshire University** **School of Design and Ceramics** Division of Ceramic Design College Road Stoke-on-Trent ST4 2DE Tel: (01782) 744531 Fax: (01782) 745627	**HND Design (Ceramics)** The course is of two years duration and offers a combination of creative, theoretical and practical learning. It is project based, supported by an extensive programme of practical skills, that include: three dimensional modelling and plaster work, print processes and ceramic manufacture. The course shares, with other ceramic courses, the finest ceramic facilities available in the UK. It has a very close relationship with the ceramic industry, which enables it to give students the benefit of a work placement which is usually in a design studio. **BA (Hons) Design (Ceramics)** This course offers a broadly based programme of study, where students initially acquire a wide range of specialist ceramic skills, before focusing on their chosen area of interest. The course shares, with our other ceramic courses the finest ceramic resources in the UK, this enables a a diverse range of work to be produced which covers all aspects of ceramic practice.
Sunderland	**University of Sunderland** **School of Arts, Design and** **Communications** Ashbourne House Ryhope Road Sunderland SR2 7EF Tel: (0191) 5152123 Fax: (0191) 5152132	**BA (Hons) 3D Design** (Glass, Architectural Glass and Ceramics) This programme has full-time and part-time modes and is a Modular Programme with Ceramics as a Core Study

WALES

Cardiff	**Cardiff Institute of** **Higher Education** **School of Design** Howard Gardens Cardiff CF2 1SP Tel: (01222) 551111	**BA (Hons) Ceramics**
Carmarthen	**Carmarthenshire College** **of Technology & Art** **Faculty of Art & Design** Job's Well Road Carmarthen Dyfed SA31 3HY Tel: (01554) 759165 Ext. 72425	**HND Design Crafts** 2 years full-time course with specialist option in ceramics: studio, casting, handbuilding and modelling. Entry by N.D.D., G.A.D., Foundation or Access. Portfolio interview in each instance
Newport	**Gwent College of Higher** **Education** **Faculty of Art & Design** College Crescent Caerleon Newport Gwent NP6 1XJ Tel: (01633) 430088 Fax: (01633) 432006	**BA (Hons) Fine Art (CNAA validated)** **BA (Hons) Graphic Design (CNAA** **validated)** Ceramics can be studied through a system of mandatory and and optional access workshops. Advanced ceramic workshop studies can be taken in year two and three in both courses. BA (Hons) Design Studies University of Wales. Ceramics is studied in year one and two and is an option in year three. Normal entry requirement for all BA courses. NB It is thought likely courses currently offered in this college will change.

Wrexham	**NE Wales Institute of Higher Education Clwyd College of Art & Design Technology** 49 Regent Street Wrexham Clwyd LL11 1PF Tel: (01978) 291 955	**BA (Hons) Art and Design** (3 year course) Modular Structure: Workshop Activity, Architectural Ceramics, Glaze Technology, Visual Studies, Cultural, Historical and Contextual Studies. The courses provides a thorough understanding of Ceramics in a theoretical and practical application. Great emphasis is placed on the enthusiasm and energy of the individual. Students have opportunity to introduce other materials within their work, and are expected to take creative risks in an atmosphere of constructive advice and criticism.

SCOTLAND

Aberdeen	**Grays School of Art** The Robert Gordons University Garthdee Road Aberdeen AB9 2QD Tel: (01224) 313247	**BA (Hons) and BA (CNAA) degrees in Design and Craft:** Ceramics/jewellery as main or subsidiary subject. Entry qualifications: 3 SCE 'H's incl. English + 2 'O's or 2 GCE 'A' incl. English + 3 'O's. Course provides opportunity of carrying out creative formal ideas which investigate two and three-dimensional composition. Techniques: thrown pottery; slab ware; handbuilding; slip-casting and press-moulding; designing and making architectural relief tiles and mural panels; methods of surface decoration; colour and glazing and kiln firing.
Dundee	**University of Dundee Duncan of Jordanstone College of Art** School of Design Perth Road Dundee DD1 4HT Tel: (01382) 23261 Fax: (01382) 201378	**Degree Course Contemporary Ceramics B.Des (Hons)** 3 years. Normally 2 'A's + 3 'O' level passes or 3 SCE 'H's + 5 'O' grade passes. Foundation or General Art Diploma. Direct entry by interview
Edinburgh	**Edinburgh College of Art** Heriot Watt University School of Design and Crafts Applied Arts Department Lauriston Place Edinburgh EH3 9DF Tel: (0131) 221 6128 Fax: (0131) 221 6004	**Degree Course/Ceramics BA (Hons)** 3 SCE 'H's incl.English , 2 SCE 'O's (C band or above). 2 GCE 'A's 3GCE 'O's (including English at 'A' or 'O'). The Section aims to provide an imput of manipulative skills and technical information running parallel to the development of each student's creative personality. Initially, set projects familiarise the students with a range of hand and machine processes applied to both form and surface design, great emphasis being place on self-programming as the course develops. Clay, glaze and kiln theory and practice are thoroughly covered, and a programme of relevant historical studies is undertaken through lectures, museum visits and personal research.

| Glasgow | **Glasgow School of Art**
167 Renfrew Street
Glasgow G3 6RQ
Tel: (0141) 353 4500 | **(BA (Hons) BA Design** Academic requirements Scottish Certificate of Education - 3 Higher Grades (including English and Art) and any other 2 subjects at 'O' Grade, OR General Certicate of Education - 2 'A' levels (including Art and English) and 3 'O' levels. If 'A' level English not obtained, passes at 'O' level required in BOTH English literature and English language. OR equivalent qualifications including HNC, HND SCOTVEC, DATEC, BTEC and Higher English. Course principally involved in clay and plaster work, but students actively encouraged to experiment with a variety of materials and techniques. |

NORTHERN IRELAND

| Belfast | **University of Ulster**
Department of Fine and
Applied Arts
York Street
Belfast BT15 1ED
Tel: (01232) 328515 | **BA (Hons) Fine Craft Design**
Study Areas: Ceramics, Silversmiths and and Jewellery, Embroidery. This provides a module-based course across the whole Faculty including Design, Fine Art, Textiles/ Fashion and Visual Communication common to all first year students. The ability to 'specialise' exists in years two and three. Equally, students may wish to extend in second and third year modules taken in first year. All courses within the Faculty allow for specialisation or for student breadth. This can permit students to undertake modules in other courses. This programme allows a student to specialise in a particular discipline. |

Post Graduate Courses in Ceramics

Aberdeen	**Grays School of Art** The Robert Gordons University Garthdee Road Aberdeen AB9 2QD Tel: (01224) 313247	**Post Graduate Diploma Ceramics** 1 year Post Graduate Diploma; BA (CNAA) or equivalent
Belfast	**University of Ulster** Department of Fine and Applied Arts York Street Belfast BT15 1ED Tel: (01232) 328515	**1 year Postgraduate Diploma** or 2 years part-time. 2 years MA or 3/4 years part-time
Cardiff	**Cardiff Institute of Higher Education** Howard Gardens Cardiff CF2 1SP Tel: (01222) 551111	**PG Dip/MA Ceramics**
Dundee	**University of Dundee** Duncan of Jordanstone College of Art School of Design Perth Road Dundee DD1 4HT Tel: (01382) 23261 Fax: (01382) 201378	**One year postgraduate M.Des.** By interview with good degree 1st or 2:1. September start.

Edinburgh	**Edinburgh College of Art** Heriot Watt University School of Design and Crafts Applied Arts Department Lauriston Place Edinburgh EH3 9DF Tel: (0131) 221 6128 Fax: (0131) 221 6004	**Postgraduate Diploma in Design** The period of study for the Postgraduate Diploma is one academic year (3 terms) and provides opportunity for well-qualified candidates to build on their undergraduate experience through further experimentation exploration and expression.
Glasgow	**Glasgow School of Art** 167 Renfrew Street Glasgow G3 6RQ Tel: (0141) 353 4500	**4-Term Masters in Design** (January - December)
London	**Middlesex University** Cat Hill Barnet Herts. EN4 8HT Tel: (0181) 362 5000 Fax: (0181) 440 9541	**Post Graduate Level** 1 year full-time or 2 years part-time MA Art and Design MA Design
	Royal College of Art Kensington Gore London SW7 2EU Tel: (0171) 584 5020	**MA/MDes./M.Phil** Ceramics & Glass 2-year courses in Designing and making Ceramics and Glass, Architectural Decoration, Design for Ceramics and Glass Industry. Research Projects in Ceramics and Glass. Materials and Technology. Entry requirements: a first degree or the equivalent experience. Competitive entrance examination February/March each year.
Stoke-on-Trent	**Staffordshire University** School of Design and Ceramics Division of Ceramic Design College Road Stoke-on-Trent ST4 2DE Tel: (01782) 744531 Fax: (01782) 745637	**Postgraduate Diploma/MA Design (Ceramics)** This linked programme of courses is primarily concerned with ceramic design for small and mass manufacture. The programme offers a one-year (34 weeks) postgraduate diploma with the opportunity for progression to either MA full-time or MA sandwich. The full-time route requires in total 53 weeks of continuous study. The sandwich route requires in total two years of full-time study which includes an industrial placement at the beginning of the second year.

Craft Potters Association 1993-94

Exhibitions

1993
Clayworks III: CPA Associate Members (February)
Heart to Heart: Pots for Valentines (February)
Robin Welch: New Ceramics (March)
The New Members Show: Keith Ashley, Bennett Cooper, Joanna Howells, Wendy Johnson, Hazel Johnston, Laurence McGowan, Jon Middlemiss, Lawson Oyekan, David White, Steve Woodhead (April)
Jane Perryman: New Work (June)
Ian Byers: New Work (July)
Setting Out: Selected Art School Graduates '93 (August)
Warren MacKenzie: New Work (October)
Gabriele Koch: New Work (October)
Boxes: Ian Byers, Emmanuel Cooper, David Frith, Jane Hamlyn, Ruth King, John Maltby, Emily Myers, Phil Rogers, Ruthanne Tudball, David White and many others (November)

1994
Fireworks 2: Craft Potters Association Professionals (January)
Pots for Valentines: Karen Bunting, Jane Hamlyn, Alan Heaps, John Maltby, John Pollex, Nicola Werner and others (February)
Martin Lewis: New Work (March)
Micki Schloessingk: New Work (May)
Josie Walter: New Work (June)
Aki Moriuchi and Sarah-Jane Selwood: New Work (July)
Setting Out: Art School Graduates (August)
David Leach: New Work (September)
Clive Bowen: New Work (October)
Playing With Fire (November)
Candlesticks: (November)

Events and Meetings 1993-94
Organised by the Members and Associates Advisory Committee

1993
Michael Casson - Lecture/Slides on 'Change and Development'. Linnean Society, London (February)
Richard Phethean - Lecture/ Slides/Exhibition 'Work and Influences'. Linnean Society, London and afterwards at Contemporary Ceramics, Marshall Street (March)
CPA and South Wales Potters: Joint Meeting at Bristol Museum - Gallery talk 'Bristol tin glaze and early hard paste porcelain'. View 'Fired Earth: History of Tiles' - touring exhibition (April)
Museum of Mankind Study Day - Archive Collection of African/Pre-Columbian Pottery at Warehouse in Shoreditch, London (May)
Jane Perryman - Lecture/Slides/Exhibition on her work - Influences and making/decoration techniques. Linnean Society, London and afterwards at Contemporary Ceramics, Marshall Street (June)

274

Peter Lane - Talk/Slides/Demonstration on 'Photographing Ceramics'. Linnean Society, London (September)
Chelsea Crafts Fair - CPA Group Visit (October)
Peter Beard - Talk/Slides 'Eygpt and After'. Linnean Society, London (November)

1994
Mo Jupp - Talk/Slides 'Ceramic Sculpture'. Linnean Society, London (February)
Joint CPA/Midland Potters Meeting. - Lectures on Henry Bergen and 'Firing the last Bottle Kiln at Longton'. View - reserve collection. Stoke on Trent Museum and Art Gallery (March)
Tour of Islamic Gallery with specialist curator. Victoria and Albert Museum, London (May)
CPA/South Wales Potters Joint Meeting - Talk by curator Barley Roscoe and view reserve studio collection: Holburne Museum and Craft Study Centre, Bath. (June)
Of Earth and Fire - Summer Ceramics Fair at Rufford Abbey (June)
AGM with Ruthanne Tudball - talk/slides 'Soda Glazed Ceramics'. Quaker Meeting House, London (July)
Guided Tour by Curator of Medieval Slipware. Victoria and Albert Museum, London (September)
CPA/East Anglian Potters Joint Meeting. Fitzwilliam Museum, Cambridge (October)

Craft Potters Association of Great Britain Ltd.

Council 1994
Chair	Phil Rogers
Vice-Chair	Jack Doherty
Hon. Secretary	Liz Gale
	Peter Beard, Emmanuel Cooper, Eileen Lewenstein Gaynor Lindsell, Jane Perryman, John Wheeldon
Associate Representative	Elizabeth Smith
CPA News Representative	Chris Speyer
Accounts	Christopher Mezzetti

Contemporary Ceramics
Craft Potters Shop and Gallery
Manager	Marta Donaghey
Assistant	Ruth Ballard

Ceramic Review
Editors	Eileen Lewenstein, Emmanuel Cooper
Editorial Assistant, Advertising	Daphne Matthews
Subscriptions and Books	Marilyn Kopkin
Assistant	John Brooksbank

Useful Addresses

Craft Potters Association
21 Carnaby Street
London W1V 1PH

Crafts Council
44a Pentonville Road
London N1 9BY

Welsh Arts Council
Holst House
9 Museum Place
Cardiff CF1 3NX

Scottish Arts Council
12 Manor Place
Edinburgh

Design Council
QED Centre
Main Avenue
Treforest Estate
Treforest CF37 5YR

Design Council
Business Design Centre
39 Corporation Street
Belfast BT1 3BA

Design Council
28 Haymarket
London SW1Y 4SU

Contemporary Applied Arts
43 Earlham Street
London WC2H 9LD

Ceramic Review
21 Carnaby Street
London W1V 1PH

Rural Development Commission
141 Castle Street
Salisbury
Wiltshire SP1 3TP

Regional Arts Boards

Arts Board North West
12 Harter Street
Manchester M1 6HY

Eastern Arts
Cherry Hinton Hall
Cambridge CB1 4DW

East Midlands Arts
Mountfields House
Forest Road
Loughborough LE11 3HU

London Arts Board
Elme House
133 Long Acre
London WC2E 9AF

Northern Arts
10 Osborne Terrace
Newcastle-upon-Tyne NE2 1NZ

South East Arts
10 Mount Ephraim
Tunbridge Wells TN4 8AS

Southern Arts
13 Clement Street
Winchester SO23 3DQ

South West Arts
Bradninch Place
Gandy Street
Exeter EX4 3LS

West Midlands Arts
82 Granville Street
Birmingham B1 2LH

Yorkshire & Humberside Arts
21 Bond Street
Dewsbury WF13 1AX

Potters

Tenth Edition

Fully revised and updated, 'Potters' is the directory of Fellows and Professional Members of the Craft Potters Association. Photographs show fine examples of Members' work, while illustrations of the potters in their studios place this in context. Addresses of all Members enable people to plan visits to potters and see where and how they work. The section 'Becoming a Potter' has been updated and is an invaluable guide to the many ways of learning the craft. Useful addresses and a record of the activities of the CPA complete this useful and informative guide.

A Ceramic Review Publication

Ceramic Review Publications

CR Publications publishes the highly successful and influential bi-monthly magazine **Ceramic Review**. This survey of modern studio ceramics covers a wide variety of topics such as making techniques, firing, glazing, marketing and history as well as providing news, reviews and comment. Essential reading for all interested in ceramics.

Clay and Glazes The Ceramic Review Book of Clay Bodies and Glaze Recipes including over 700 recipes from established potters. An excellent source for all potters.

Potters Tips Compiled by Robert Fournier from tips submitted by potters to *Ceramic Review*, Potters Tips is full of useful information whether building kilns, mixing clay or caring for the environment.

Full details from Ceramic Review Publications, 21 Carnaby Street, London W1V 1PH

CONTEMPORARY CERAMICS

CRAFT POTTERS
SHOP AND GALLERY

POTS   BOOKS   TOOLS   EXHIBITIONS

CONTEMPORARY
CERAMICS
7 MARSHALL STREET
LONDON . W1

OPEN MONDAY - SATURDAY 10-5.30pm THURSDAY 10-7pm

TELEPHONE 0171-437 7605